THE BEN

IF YOU DON'T READ THIS BOOK...

You may be new to sales or professional salesperson with 35 years selling experience, the question is, the next time you want to sell your product or increase your profitability, will you be able to do it?

You may not even be selling anything, but you just want to be able have more influence and control over the situations you're in. But without knowing the techniques taught in *The Secret to Sales Success* your powers of persuasion will be less than they could be and you will get your way less often. Once you know the secret, you will sell more effectively.

The truth is we're always trying to sell quite a number of ideas, beliefs and opinions and we want others to agree with us. We all want our point of view to win more often with members of our family, associations, neighbors, and with our friends and prospects. Are you completely happy with how are you doing this now? Would you like to improve your ability to persuade people and sell product?

If you care about becoming sales professional or you want to develop your persuasion skills for political, social, or environmental cause, you need to understand the simple secrets of *The Secret to Sales Success*. There's no reason for you to invest a tremendous amount of time and effort and not reap the rewards you deserve. And just like a surgeon would never perform an operation without training, understanding the secrets of how to conduct a successful sales presentation will provide you with the tools necessary to advance your cause, or your career.

Failure is a thing of the past, you've taken the first step towards improving your ability to sell, your powers of persuasion, and your ability to generate higher income by applying the principles that you learn in this book.

Every technique in this book has proven its value in real sales situations by tremendously successful sales professionals. Each technique will provide you with a new dimension of effectiveness designed to help you move your sales career forward.
Take a moment to review the contents from some of the pages deeper in this book, and then decide.

Can you afford to face tomorrow without all the aid this book gives you?

If you want to close more sales,
If you want to achieve higher profits,
If you want to be more organized,
If you want to enjoy people more,
If you want to have more influence,
If you want your opinion to be valued more,
If you want to work smarter not harder,

Take this book home with you tonight.

Chris Evans

The Secret to Sales Success

PROVIDING THE KEY TO PROSPERITY AND A
BETTER LIFE FOR EVERY SALES PROFESSIONAL

Chris Evans

Kings Hill Publishing
PO 2870
Malibu, CA 990265

Kimgs Hill Publishing is an imprint of Evans Sales Solutions, Inc.
The Kings Hill Publishing name and logo is a trademark of Evans
Sales Solutions, Inc.

Printed in the United States of America

First published edition: August 2011

Once again I need to thank my wife Rebekah for her unconditional support and motivation to bring this book to fruition. Thank you to Jamison, Chris II and Sagan. I appreciate the support you show me each day.

A special thanks to Dave Dowler for his guidance and inspiration.

Finally, I want to acknowledge *Tom Hopkins* who's training has allowed me to grow in the sales profession and in life. Without the training and information Tom shares so freely I would not be able to tour the world and conduct the training sessions that I do.

Tom's dedication to helping salespeople become more professional has enriched the lives of thousands as it has mine.

CHAPTERS

"Cannibals prefer those who have no spines."
Stanislaw Lem – Author (1921 – 2006)

Chapter 1 – No Fear

I believe there is good in the world. In fact, *I know* there is good in the world. You can see it every day if you look around. Interestingly enough, it's never the good of the bombastic or famous that gets my attention. There seems to be something phony when our politicians start doing great things just before elections or when they just happen to feed the homeless with 30 photographers in tow. Don't get me wrong, it's very nice when Brad Pitt and Angelina Jolie give one million dollars to help tornado victims, but it's just as nice when an anonymous person drops off clothing at a Salvation Army or one person simply telephones another person and cheers them up after they experienced a challenging time. It's all-good.

Unfortunately, if we're going to have good, we must also have evil. There is some truth to the saying that in order to know the good times, you must have some bad times; but when you think about it, even that statement minimizes the effect of evil. We don't call them evil times, we call them bad or tough times. Maybe because it's easier for us to cope with evil when we don't call it by its real name, but evil exists and very often runs rampant across the world.

Most days, evil seems to be a lot easier to find than good. We have newspapers, television news, the internet, and multiple forms of information distribution that have made it their goal to trumpet as much of the evil in the world as possible. They have learned that evil sells. Splash the front page of the paper with a four-color picture of the latest psycho killer and you're sure to sell more papers. Feature a picture of someone handing a dollar to a person down on his or her luck and nobody seems to care. That won't sell papers.

As a professional salesperson, I believe we have tremendous powers. We have the power to do good by helping people and we also have the power to do evil by hurting people. Great salespeople do good things every day of the week, but it's rarely the kind of good that gets recognized. When you help a prospect find exactly what they need to fill whatever need they have, you have done good. This is one of the things I love about selling. It's just as if the salesperson can be any super hero they want to be. They get to decide whether they are going to be a super hero or a super villain. But I think it goes much deeper than that.

I believe as humans it's our job to challenge evil and when possible stop it. Almost every day we encounter evil. It can be as simple and destructive as gossip about a fellow worker or obvious evil when we find a co-worker stealing time, cash, or supplies from our employer. It's evil; remember if you're going to be a super hero, you're on call twenty-four hours a day. One reason evil is as prevalent as it is, is because potential super heroes stand by and allow evil to happen. They must think their shift is over, but fighting evil is a tough twenty-four hour a day job and it's not easy.

The world as we know it is continually finding new ways to let evil prevail. It's become unfashionable and even frowned upon by some segments of society for you to express your beliefs unless you agree with whatever vocal minority is speaking at the moment. The new tolerance movement promotes the belief that you should be tolerant of everyone and everything. It's cool and correct to be tolerant; but if you have a different opinion or don't agree with the enlightened tolerant ones, you won't be tolerated.

I've always been the type of person that resists the normal ebb and flow of social movement. It seems that quite often I'm on the outside looking in. For many years, my wife would warn me about crossing the line. I know she wondered why I did some of the things I did. It wasn't until she realized that the reason I don't worry about crossing the line is because I don't have a line. It's impossible for me to cross something that doesn't exist. It's just easier for me to not worry about the politically correct view and to express my view. If you don't agree with me, it's ok. We don't have to destroy each other. We just don't agree.

We Must Conquer Evil

There's tons of stuff I don't understand. I can't understand how the same people, who will rally, march and cheer for a "Woman's Right To Choose," will also work to strip away a smoker's right to smoke. It's ok to vacuum a living fetus out your vagina for the sake of convenience, but you can't inhale someone else's passing smoke? Does that make sense?

I'll never understand how an environmentalist will scream about preserving a beautiful piece of land, but not want to buy it from the landowner who bought it and is paying the taxes. It's easier to restrict someone else's right to do what they want on their land than it is to simply buy it and let it sit empty. I understand the environmentalist may not have the money, but whose fault is that? The environmental movement today appears to be a ship without a rudder, yet it's the flavor of the month with hundreds of companies rushing to prove how environmentally conscious they are. No one knows where they are going, but they are going there very fast.

I spent four years as an elected member of our local city council. I found it uncomfortable when people came forward and thanked us for all agreeing to a particular issue and voting on it without dissent. I was nervous that we hadn't considered everything. Some people loved it when the council called an issue and then either approved it or turned it down five to zero. They saw it as a sign that the council was moving in unison. I believed the role of the council was to discuss debate and learn about an issue and then vote your conscience. Most of the time (particularly on development issues), people would come forward, express their opinion and then accuse you of being dishonest and a developer's patsy if you didn't agree with them. It didn't matter that half the time they had bad information. If you pointed out the fact that they had old or wrong information, they hated you even more. Knowing that I was a public figure, people my company did business with would threaten to write letters to the paper if you had a business dispute and they could say anything they wanted. It didn't have to be true. My position was simple – take your best shot, I didn't care what they said or what they threatened.

We once had a gentleman come forward to speak on a development issue. He was the city planner from a nearby city who happened to reside in our city. As an employee of a city government, he understood the "system." At this particular meeting, he was speaking against a large housing project that had gone through years of hearings and millions of dollars in required reports. He had found that 50 years ago there had been an oil well on the 4,000-acre project. All of the environmental reports indicated that the oil well had long since been capped and there weren't any safety concerns; yet when he came forward, he claimed that the oil well had not been capped properly (as if he had any way to make that assumption) and that because oil had cancer causing agents in it and the project was going to have families with children playing outside, we as a city council would state that we didn't care whether children got cancer if we approved the project.

After the meeting, I approached him and said, "Do you know the information you have is wrong?" He said, "Oh, I know, but that's the way the game is played. In tomorrow's paper what do you think it's going to say?" He gave me a smirk, said I was an asshole and walked off.

For the next six months, we had a steady stream of people who didn't want the project approved reference the fact that the council had been warned about cancer risks and why weren't we listening to the facts about cancer causing agents on the property?

It was pointless to tell them we were listening to the facts, just not the lies put forward by people who didn't care about the truth. When enough good people stand by and allow evil to run rampant, evil temporarily wins.

I sat on the far right in the council chamber and a gentleman named Bernardo Perez, sat on the far left. I'm sure it was a coincidence, but that was also how our political views tended to land. On numerous occasions, Bernardo and I would debate issues from opposite sides. We even had some fairly heated discussions from time to time. Our council meetings were televised and it seems many people enjoyed watching us go at it. In fact, it wasn't uncommon for people to approach me and say, "You must hate Bernardo Perez." I'm sure the same happened to him about me. What people didn't know was that many times prior to a meeting I would pick Bernardo up; we would eat dinner or grab a cup of coffee and then drive to the meeting together. After the meeting, we would drive home together. Not once during my time on the city council did I ever feel anything other than respect for Bernardo. He was doing his job to the best of his ability. When he ran for Mayor I worked on his campaign. He's still a good friend many years later. We look at the political world differently, but we respect each other. We both stood up for what we believed, but we never diluted ourselves into believing that the other person was ever doing anything but their best. The other thing I think politicians need to remember is that they are temporary. The public is there forever, but the person who's Mayor today probably won't be Mayor in a few years.

Recently, evil has taken on the penis. That's right, even the penis can't escape the evil nature of a few demented people with determination. It seems a group in San Francisco has decided that circumcision is wrong and they want to pass a law outlawing circumcision. Never mind the fact that some religions have required circumcision for thousands of years. This small group of elitists has decided that they should make the rules for everyone else and they don't like circumcision. I find it interesting that in a city where about half the population loves the penis and the other half hates it, the penis has grown into such a concern. The point is there will always be a group of people who believe they know better than you do how to run your life. I'll bet some of the same people who believe it is their job to tell you what you can and cannot do with your newborn son's penis believe their bedroom is their castle and no one should tell them what they can and can't do in their bedroom. They believe they are so enlightened that they know far better than you what can be done. Salespeople deal with tyranny every day.

Dodging Land Mines

Salespeople have to dodge the land mines of evil and they can't have fear for repercussions. It appears that many professional salespeople have fallen for the misconception that in order to be good at what you do you can't stand for anything. You have to morph your presentation, life, and attitude into one giant homogeneous blob that simply moves forward, turning out sales no matter what the situation or environment. If you have an opinion, defy evil or express a view, it might cost you sales; so the best thing to do is to please everyone all the time, as if not getting a sale every now and then because you had some moral character is a bad thing.

I can promise you, if you express an opinion, have standards and live by them, it's going to cost you sales. It's going to happen because that's the way evil works. Just as the villain challenges the hero, evil is going to challenge you. But what would happen if the minute Mr. Freeze punched Batman in the face, Batman would run away? Mr. Freeze would win and Gotham City would be doomed. The truth is Batman gets knocked down quite a bit. Some people even hate Batman and think he's the criminal, but does Batman care? Hell no, Batman always stands for good and he ultimately wins.

You can be Batman and yes, in this politely correct world, Batwoman. But it's going to have a price. Just as I believe that

God made us and through his son Jesus gave us a way to conquer evil, I believe that we as humans have to go out of our way to promote good. No fear of failure, no fear of evil situations, and certainly no fear of other people. It's not about denominations or church attendance; it's about good vs. evil.

As a professional salesperson, the chances are very strong that eventually someone will mention you on the Internet in some review web site. One interesting thing about the proliferation of Internet sites like Yelp and Yahoo Local and others that allow you to rate the services is that people who now have the protection of anonymity have all become reviewers. People who in the past would have just forgotten about the fact that the ice cream cone had a crack in it now have a way to transpose their sorry lives onto anyone who crosses their paths. As reviewers, they all believe their opinion counts; and as authors, they know no bounds. There's no infraction that doesn't deserve a righteous tone of indignation. If you are a business and you don't offer 300% of what you should for 50% of the price, you're sure to have reviews that are bad and I've seen people try to instill fear in businesses and salespeople by threatening bad ratings.

Some people simply don't understand that their kids can't fly the plane or they can't get the extra discount after the coupon expired. They go home, sit at the computer and let the evil spew. From the -15 star rating they give, you would have thought the business wanted to molest their child. Then you read the entire review and find out the restaurant was busy, they didn't have a reservation and they had to wait. The information age has created the situation we find ourselves in, but I also believe that there are so many whacko reviews that people have already started discounting what they read. The Internet rating sites want us to believe that 50% of the people follow online reviews. I think the number is much lower than that.

Even without the rating sites, we live in an information world. I recently helped at a charity event where people had an opportunity to make reservations in advance and tour an active

US Navy Destroyer. There were about 200 seats available for a tour of the ship throughout the weekend and due to security you had to order tickets in advance and be pre-screened by the Navy. For some reason, they didn't want just anyone walking around a ship with nuclear warheads which seemed reasonable to me.

While the vast majority of people who came without reservations hoping to take a tour understood, there was a small group of individuals who were simply evil about getting on the ship. One person after the other would show up, tell us why they were more important than everyone else and why they should get a seat. It was simply evil behavior after evil behavior from this small group of people. They incorrectly assumed that if they threatened, cajoled and bullied the volunteers on the dock, they would get their way. If that had happened, evil would have won; but because the volunteers and the Navy stood their ground, they didn't get on board. In short order, there were letters of protest in the papers and the organizers received nasty emails. Evil doesn't like to lose.

In both life and the sales occupation, if you're going to fight against evil, you can't have fear. I actually had the phrase, "No Fear" tattooed on my right arm in Kanji and it's amazing. The minute I adopted the theme of no fear, a bunch of scary stuff started happening. It was as if once I decided to live without fear, evil decided to challenge me. Honestly, it's a day-to-day struggle, but the point I'm trying to make is that we all have the ability to decide if we are going to stand up for what's right and possibly be outside our comfort level or if we are going to stand inside the crowd and follow along with the status quo.

People in the world today have learned that evil has no boundaries and the righteous have no balls. The vast majority of the time, people who are "right" somehow feel that by showing restraint and not fighting evil just as ferociously as evil fights them, they are somehow better off. The meek may inherit the earth, but I'm only going to be on earth a short time. I have no idea what I would do with it if I did inherit it. You never seem to find leaders in the middle of the flock. They are the ones out front, taking the hits and leading the rest. Be a leader!

Speaking of being a bold leader with no fear, let me challenge you.

Right now, I want you to call Donald Trump and let him know your services are available. Do you think it's ridiculous? I'll bet "the Donald," buys cars or insurance. I'll bet he needs Internet services or marketing. Furthermore, of all the people you see on television, I'll bet he appreciates initiative and bold leadership more than most. After all, he's a prospect. Why not call him? Is Donald Trump so special that we need to fear calling him on the phone? Just to help out, I'm going to do the hard part. Here's his office phone number, 212-832-2000.

Before you ask, I'll tell you. I called the number, but I'm not going to tell you what happened. After you call, send me an email and tell me what happened. Remember, No Fear!

Many people believe sales is an easy job with little training required, but I believe they don't understand what being a true sales professional is. The true sales professional stands between the customer and the shyster who would take their money and deliver the wrong product. The true sales professional has morals and standards which dictate that he or she will never do something that hurts the client. The true sales professional fights evil every time they come across it, and they don't let those that are emboldened by their idiocy have their way simply because they scream loud. The ones that are typically screaming the loudest are typically the ones that are the most insecure. Be secure.

No Fear

As a professional salesperson you are a leader. It's up to you to lead your prospects and customers in the honest pursuit of helping them fill their needs. I've found that often it's the sale professional that makes the product decision, not the customer. The sales professional listens to what the client wants or what they want to achieve and then shows the customer what they have that will fill their need. In effect, the salesman decided the Whirlpool 8550 microwave oven was what the customer needed and the customer simply agreed. The salesperson is the one with all the super powers.

My pastor once said he didn't want to convince people to believe in God. He explained that if you're the type of person that can be convinced there is a God; someone else can convince you that there isn't one. The weak link in the chain is the person being convinced. You either have faith and a belief that grows, or you don't. I feel the same is true when it comes to sales. If you have to convince someone to buy your product, someone else can convince them not to. There has to be a mutual understanding that the product is what the prospect needs and will achieve its stated purpose. Once the professional salesperson has done that they are a hero to that client, and there won't be any need for fear.

In 1980, I had an opportunity to work for a very short time at Lincoln National Life Insurance. What I learned in that nine-month period could fill another book, but I remember one sales professional named Terry Murphy. I had found a potential client with about $25,000 to invest in an annuity, and at the time I knew nothing about annuities. I asked Terry to go with me because he was one of the most seasoned agents in the office and widely recognized as an annuities expert.

The potential client's name was Mr. Fox. During the time that Terry and I were at Mr. Fox's house, we found out that he actually had quite a bit more than the $25,000 he wanted to invest. I was excited because the commission on the sale would be about $4,000 each and I could really use the money. The three of us hit it off and, after an hour or so of fact finding, Terry was closing the sale. As he was filling in the paperwork he said, "You know, I just remembered that we have another program that might be better for you. It doesn't pay a commission and has no load (fees), but I think in your situation it's going to be better for you." I was ready to die. Did he really just give away $8,000 in commission? He was 75% done with the application and Mr. Fox had his checkbook on the table!

During the drive back to the office I was livid. As a young, starving sales professional, I needed that sale. Terry explained. First, we have the sale. From that perspective we were successful. Second, at some point in the future, Mr. Fox will be in a different situation and he will need a product that pays a commission. When that happens we will split the commissions earned, but Terry wasn't going to put Mr. Fox into anything that wasn't first and foremost good for Mr. Fox. Terry believed he could always make money, but his higher calling was protecting his clients and making sure they made money. That's why he was so successful. He explained that the way he slept at night was never putting a client into a situation he wouldn't want his wife and kids to be in if he weren't around. If that meant he wouldn't see any money from Mr. Fox, it was fine. He had done the right thing.

As a footnote to this story, I left Lincoln National Life and moved on to other opportunities. Several years later, I received a $6,000 check in the mail from Terry. He added a note saying, "Here's your half of the sale. Mr. Fox just moved his money into an annuity that pays commission." Let me ask you, is that integrity or not? Do you think that one of the reasons Terry might be blessed the way he has been is that he fights evil every day? I learned a valuable lesson from Terry on the night we drove 60 miles for no money, and I learned another valuable lesson several years later.

There is good in the world and we don't need to fear evil.

"Don't be humble… You're not that great."
Golda Meir – Prime Minister of Israel (1898 – 1978)

Chapter 2 – Your Attention Please

Many times, I start reading a book and if the content doesn't grab my attention almost immediately, I put the book down and may not come back to it at a later date. I find it frustrating when an author has so little to say that they spend the first 12 chapters building up to that one big idea or interesting point that they're trying to make. My philosophy when conducting business seminars or helping sales professionals has always been to provide them with as much information as possible as quickly as possible. This book is no different.

How many times have you attended a seminar or purchased a book and after you were done with that said, "I learned one good idea for my investment, so it was worth it"? I believe that when people attend my seminars or read my books they should walk away with not just one good idea, but with many good ideas. If, when you're done with this book, you believe you've only received one good idea, I'm going to consider that failure on my part.

To that end, I want to start in the very beginning by giving you a big idea. It's very simple, but yet I'll bet you've been told exactly the opposite over the years. I'll have several of these assumptions throughout this book. I call these "Evans Truisms." Fundamental facts that I believe are important for you to know and agree with, in order to be successful.

I must admit, sometimes I feel like I've slipped into an alternate universe. I attend seminars or round tables and I listen to experts speak about one topic or another, and they always seem to make things sound so hard. They will go on for 30 minutes explaining some simple concept that's only become hard to understand because they don't know what they are talking about, or they want it to seem so hard that everyone has to look at them as the Grand PooPah of knowledge on whatever topic these blow holes are covering. It's just not that hard and a stupid idea is a stupid idea no matter how long it takes to explain it. Maybe that's why I try to keep everything as short as possible.

Evans Truism Number One
Sales Is Not a Numbers Game.

Over the years, I've had countless sales managers, sales trainers, and other sales professionals routinely remind me that sales is a numbers game. The more leads or prospects you pump into the top of the funnel, the more sales will drop out of the bottom of the funnel. I once had a sales manager who really didn't sell anything and didn't really manage very well either. He had simply outlasted all of the other sales professionals, so because of seniority he became sales manager. In our weekly sales training meetings, he would bring in some canned presentation or make us sit and watch a video because he believed that was the way to get his sales force pumped up and motivated. He would end each meeting by reminding us that sales is a numbers game and to be successful you had to be in the game. His theory went something like this.

- Find tons of people or businesses that may be prospects.
- Put them into your sales cycle.
- Harass them until they give you an appointment.
- Conduct the appointment and pressure them to buy.
- Close a fraction of the original number of prospects.
- Do it again.

My Sales Manager believed that you just did the numbers. If it took 1,000 prospects to make 10 sales and you wanted 100 sales, you would simply need to have 10,000 prospects.

I find it hard to believe that it took me nine months to figure out this is simply utter nonsense and this guy didn't know the first thing about prospecting, let alone selling. It's insanity to assume that because you can identify thousands of cold prospects, you have an opportunity to sell them your product.

I'll bet you have run across sales managers who have said the same thing to you. Or you've attended a workshop where they explain the importance of finding as many leads as you can and converting them to prospects as quickly as possible. Maybe you've even bought into this theory, thinking that the more people you contact, the more money you're going to make.

The major problem with nonsense like this is the same problem that most multi-level marketing companies have. Virtually every multi-level organization has approached me at one time or another and it always seems to be a similar story. Most told me how their wonderful new product will solve a major problem, or cure cancer, or clean toilets better than anything ever cleaned before. Then they tell me a story about how the inventor of the product has chosen to bring the product to market via a network marketing company rather than through conventional channels because they are so committed to helping people take control of their lives and make millions of dollars. These *gods of business* have an unshakable belief that network marketing is going to provide "you" with an unbeatable opportunity to pocket millions of dollars; you simply have to find three people and help them find three people and so on…

It never seems to occur to these people to figure out what number of people it would truly take for them to be successful. They work on the theory that sales is a numbers game. Grab as many people as you can, shove them into your sales system and, eventually, you'll have more sales than you can handle. If you find 30 people, surely 3 will get motivated and work hard. Then they can find their 3 out of 30 and on it goes. A quick look at the math shows that you have to contact about 72,900,000 people within the first 5 levels. Go ahead and try for level 6 and you have to be talking with just about everyone on the planet.

Many years ago, I was talked into attending a "motivational meeting" held by a new multi-level company. At the meeting, the leader talked about this great new product called Aspartame. At the time, it was the first artificial sweetener that didn't taste like chalky molasses. The leader explained how the world was dying for artificial sweetener and the inventor had chosen their multi-level company to bring it to the world. I asked at the meeting if it truly made sense that they would be the only company in the galaxy with this new product. The leader assured me that it was the company's commitment to mom and pop businesses that prevented them from selling it to anyone outside the networking organization.

I didn't believe him for a second. It just didn't make sense. The inventor was going to turn away every major food company in the world to distribute their product through a pyramid of people meeting in people's garages. It was silly. Sure enough, about a month after the meeting, a large company like Nabisco or Pillsbury announced they had this great new product called Aspartame. All the people who had invested $1,250 to be distributors were stuck. Don't get me wrong, I do participate in some multi-level organizations. *Send Out Cards* has been a great organization. I use the product and occasionally someone I know uses it as well. For a while, I used *Hello World* and it was great, but I never register for the services assuming I'm going to capture the world and make a billion dollars. If they have a good product I can use to help my customers, I join and use the product.

The truth is sales is not a numbers game. Sales is a qualifying game. You definitely need people to talk to. But more importantly than just talking to anyone, you need to be sure to talk to qualified individuals who need your product.

Let's say you are selling siding for a home. You don't prospect in an apartment complex. Why not? Because it's obvious that people living in apartments will not be buying siding. Sure, you may run into someone who knows someone who needs siding, but for every 1,000 doors you knock on there is going to be a very small percentage of people who need siding for a home. It's much more productive to work in an area of homes that were built 25 to 30 years ago than it is to prospect through an apartment complex. Clearly, using this example, sales is not a numbers game.

I'll bet the same is true in whatever industry you're in. Insurance representatives can reach out and contact literally millions of people, and at the end of the day they will have simply exerted effort on millions of unproductive leads. If they focused on just a few hundred individuals that had an insurance policy renewal, within the next few months they would be much more productive than trying to promote their product to millions of people. Again, it's very clear, sales is not a numbers game.

I want to caution you. As you read through the book, there will be many times when we will be teaching things that are unconventional and go against the day-to-day belief of many sales managers. You may not want to go to work tomorrow morning and try and explain to a sales manager who believes sales is a numbers game that it's not. You're much better off becoming the top salesperson in your company, and when they come to you and ask, "How did you do it?" you can explain to them what you know. Many sales managers are nice people, but lousy salesmen. In fact, many sales managers became managers so they don't have to sell any more, yet they get to keep a level of responsibility and prestige that they desire.

A Request

I'd like to start with one simple request, and this request comes from years of experience in teaching sales professionals. I request that as you read this book, whenever possible, you do it in a way that you cannot be interrupted. I want you to be able to read the material and think about it as you're reading it. To that end, I would ask that you turn your cell phone off just as if you were at a seminar.

Let's face it, many people believe that their cell phone is their umbilical cord and their participation in their business is so important that if they are not available within seconds to anyone who needs them, their whole business will collapse. How many times have you returned to the office or to your home because you forgot your cell phone? Many of us act like we believe we need to be instantly available all the time, but in our mind we all know that's not true. More likely, the adage "everyone is replaceable" is true. If while reading this book you turn your cell phone off and you spend 30 minutes focusing on the material, I promise your business will not fall apart. Your life will not come to an end and the world will continue to rotate just as it has for 4.5 billion years. However, your ability to focus more clearly on the material is going to help you absorb the information and get a much better result from this book.

- Let's start with some very simple questions.
- Are you happy?
- Do you receive enjoyment from what you do?
- If you were able to do anything, what would it be?
- What's your idea of success?

As I've worked with sales professionals, I found that many of them have many different ideas of what success is. There are almost as many definitions of success as there are people on the planet, so it makes it a little difficult when someone says, "I want to be successful."

Some people measure success by the material possessions they and others own. I have a friend who believes success is having his own airplane and being able to travel whenever he wants. In his mind, he knew he was successful the day he purchased his very first plane. As his success grew so did the size of his plane.

For many of the people that know him, as well as for many of his clients, it's one of the first things they mention when they talk about him. They will say, "You know, Jeff owns a plane." As if owning the plane is Jeff's major achievement in life. Now Jeff has a wonderful wife, great kids, and lives in a beautiful home; but because his definition of success is having a plane, other people have tuned into his yardstick or the way he measures things and now measure his success the same way he does.

Others believe success is measured by how they help others. The amount of money they donate to charity or how much they give to their church is how they measure whether they are successful or not. These individuals go out of their way to reinvest as much of their time and money as possible, many times because it makes them feel better about themselves.

I have noticed, now more than ever, that many of the politicians who represent us spend a significant amount of time apologizing to the rest of the world for the United States of America's success. It seems as though they believe that most of the things that are going wrong in the world are, because the United States has been successful. Without the significant leadership and money invested by the United States of America, the world would be a very different place and frankly, I don't understand how the same people who beg for our votes feel the need to denigrate our country when dealing with the rest of the world.

If you measure success by how much you help others, I want to make you aware of a great organization called *Kiva.com*; *Kiva.com* allows you to loan people throughout the world money in $25 increments. It's a super way to help people in need and I'm proud to have several micro-loans out at all times.

There are also people who measure success by the amount of time they can spend with their family. I recently did some consulting work for a gentleman who was privileged enough to be very successful in business very early in life. He now has the luxury of working on projects that he enjoys, rather than working on projects he must do to make an income. He sets aside time every single day to spend with his children, his wife, and his business, and of those three things the business is the last thing that receives his time. Now, I understand that most of us must go out each and every day and make a living. We don't have the luxury of not working, but I hope to reveal to you, in the following pages, a way that we can truly define success however you may do that, make your life more enjoyable, more profitable, and help you enjoy a much longer life because it will be stress-free.

I once received a card for Father's Day. On the card was a saying I had seen before, and in fact I had tried to share this with others, but I couldn't remember the exact words. The card was titled

The Essence of Survival

Every morning in Africa, a gazelle wakes up. It knows it must run faster than the fastest lion or it will be killed... Every morning a lion wakes up. It knows it must outrun the slowest gazelle or it will starve to death. It doesn't matter whether you're a lion or a gazelle... When the sun comes up, you'd better be running.

I've known many sales people over the years. Better yet, I've known many people who called themselves sales professionals. Many of the people I met who called themselves sales professionals were not sales professionals at all. You see, I believe the true sales professional can be defined by their actions and not by how much product they sell.

Many years ago, *Tom Hopkins* taught me what I believe is the perfect definition of what a salesperson is. It's important information so I'll repeat it.

A salesperson is somebody who helps other people make decisions that are good for them. It's just that simple. If you help other people make decisions that are good for them, then you can be a salesperson too. On the other hand, if you force people to make decisions that are bad for them, you may still call yourself a salesperson, but you're not. You're a shyster.

There's a huge difference between a professional salesperson helping someone make decisions that are good for them and a shyster forcing people to make decisions that are bad for them. By far, the vast majority of sales professionals I have met are more interested in helping other people than making money. And the truly great sales professionals I have met are always more interested in helping the client than making money. They understand that by helping the client, they are in fact going to make a lot of money.

The Mind

I want you to think for a minute about your mind and what it does. Your mind is unbelievably interesting. Think about it, your mind is working 24 hours a day. Your mind produces dreams when you're awake and it also produces dreams when you're asleep. The primary difference is when you're awake you have your eyes and your ears and a framework in which to understand the thoughts your mind is producing. At night, when you sleep, you do not have the external stimulation, so your mind tends to wander and create dreams that sometimes are very strange.

We are dreaming all the time. Well, before you were born, your mind started working and creating dreams. After your birth, your mind continued to work and slowly, over a period of years, you acquired the framework to understand what your mind is telling you. Humans are born with an unbelievable capacity to use their mind and to learn. But as we grow older and we receive more framework that establishes guidelines for us, we tend to limit what our mind can do.

Children are the best example of unlimited minds. They have the capacity to daydream, create fantasy realities and truly enjoy their imagination. It's not because we aged that our ability to live in a fantasy world became limited. It's because as we aged we learned more of the guidelines and rules and framework that limited what our mind could do. Children have much less framework and fewer rules to limit what their mind can do. As an adult, each and every single day, we take the experience we've had over the years and the framework we've learned to live within and then we apply it to the reality of that day. Truth be told, you are not the same person today you were yesterday because you have had experiences yesterday, which affected the way you act today. Children have had much less time to experience the limiting factors of life or reality, so they have the ability to use their mind and their imagination in ways that adults can only hope to remember. As we grew older, we learned that we needed to focus our mind in order to achieve certain goals.

Attention is the ability we have to focus on that which we want to perceive. We are incredible beings, we can perceive millions of things simultaneously, but what we turn our attention towards is what our mind will concentrate on.

One of the things we learned as we were growing up are the rules of society. We were told what to believe and what not to believe, what may or may not be acceptable, and what is good or bad, as well as many other rules that our parents gave us as we grew up. They shared with us from their perspective the knowledge that they had. What we did not understand at the time was that they were drawing from the experience they had, and our parents' rules limited their creative capacity. In effect, the rules that your parents had on their mind were transferred to you. And now you've taken those rules that you learned as a child, added to them the new rules from the experiences you've had as you aged and now you have your own framework, your own reality within which your mind works.

Think about it. When you were in school you concentrated on what the teacher was teaching you. Maybe you went to church, and you concentrated on what the pastor taught you. When you are home, you face the same situation with your mom and dad, and the rest your family. Each and every one of them requires a certain amount of your attention. In fact, many of your siblings would compete with you for your parents' attention. Our need for attention becomes very strong and it doesn't stop just because we're not children anymore.

So, we have limits on our mind that regulate how we think. Many people call them beliefs or morals or conditions that we live by. No matter what you call them, they are rules to control our mind and our thoughts, and in some cases they limit our ability to be successful because we've imposed them on our mind over the years. As a child, you don't have an opportunity to choose what you believe or what you don't believe; in fact, your parents or your family or the society that you live in form many of the beliefs well before you're born and then impose those beliefs upon you after you're born.

As we grew older, most of us did not rebel against those beliefs. In fact, we adopted those beliefs. That's why you often find people who become members of a certain political party because their parents were. Many people attend a church or participate in a denomination because that's the way they were raised. Most of us did not have any control when we were children over what church to go to because our parents made that decision for us. And children believe everything that adults say. They agree with them and they have faith in what their parents say. Occasionally, you will find a child who rebels against the beliefs of his parents, but that's rare. It's much more common for children to surrender their beliefs and take on the same beliefs as their parents.

As a child, if you broke the rules, you were punished; when you went along with the rules, you were rewarded. Many children were both punished and rewarded many times a day. That's why many of us has the belief system we have as adults. Please don't misunderstand, I'm not saying that raising your children and providing them with a framework of your beliefs to understand the world is a bad thing. The truth is it's simply the way the world works. It can be good, and it can be bad. We simply need to understand that many of the beliefs we hold as adults are due to the framework that was provided to us when we were children.

There are millions of people walking around the planet right now that look in the mirror and say to themselves, "I am ugly and unworthy." There are also people who walk around and say, "I am God's gift to creation, everyone should want to be me." Obviously, both of these extremes are wrong. But the reason it's important for a salesperson to understand the framework from which they were raised is because sales is one of the occupations where your attitude is very important to the outcome. Most of the times, understanding the framework from which we were raised will help us understand why we have the attitude that we do.

I hope you didn't grow up in a home where your parents continually told you that you were stupid or ugly or overweight or unsuccessful or any of the negative things that adults sometimes transpose onto children. But if you did, you need to understand that none of the negative framework you grew up with needs to impact your success in the sales profession.

Sales Attitude

It's interesting that sales is one of the few occupations that you can go to work, have a bad attitude and at the end of the day still feel like you put in a hard day's work. Let's face it, the only other place where you can have a bad attitude all day long, provide poor service to the customer and still get paid at the end of the month is a government employee. Anyone who's been to the Department of Motor Vehicles at any point in their life understands most of the people that work at the DMV are not there because they have an overwhelming desire to provide great customer service to their fellow man. In fact, most of the time when you show up to the DMV you feel like a repressed person. You sit quietly and wait until someone decides to look into whatever issue you may have.

But imagine for a minute that you are a cashier at a grocery store. You go to work at 7 AM and unfortunately, because of whatever may have happened at home the night before, you have a poor attitude. You punch in at work and go to your register and start your day. But because you have a bad attitude that day you decide you're only going to put in 50% effort. The first customer puts their items on the belt and you start swiping them across the scanner, but because you have a bad attitude you're only swiping every other item. You fill up the customer's bag of groceries and send them on their way, knowing that you only put in a 50% effort and they only paid half the price that your employer was owed. How long do you think you would keep that job? Obviously, the answer is not long. The minute your employer found out he would terminate your employment and you would be truly having a bad day.

But in sales, it doesn't work that way. For some reason, many of the same weak sales managers who have professed for years that sales is a numbers game also believe that 90% of the battle is keeping your attitude positive so that you can do your job. A grocery store manager likes it when his cashiers have a good attitude; but frankly, they can be having the worst day of their life. And as long as they scan the groceries across the scanner and collect the right amount of money, then return the right amount of change, those cashiers will keep their job. It's only in sales that we are allowed to use the crutch that we're just not into it or that our performance is poor because other things are impacting our life.

True professional salespeople have enough experience and knowledge to understand that as long as they do the right thing at the right time they can sell in any situation. I understand it's always easier to sell when you're happy and you have a good attitude; but 95% of the population can sell when they're happy and have a good attitude. It takes a sales professional to sell when they're not happy, have chaos in their life and there are things going on around them that they can't control. A true professional salesperson can get up each and every day, clear their mind of the useless clutter or negative framework they were subjected to as a child, and go out, meet people, present a concept or product or service, and close sales. If you're an employer, you don't need people who only know how to sell when times are good.

If you're a salesperson, your employer doesn't need you when the selling is easy. What truly separates professionals from amateurs when it comes to selling is their ability to sell in any situation, no matter what is going on around them in the world or what is going on in their home life. If they can still show up each and every single day and work towards a goal of success by closing sales, just like an automated selling machine, they will be successful.

Evans Truism Number Two
Every day is a bright new day with all kinds of possibilities.

For most of their lives, I have woken up my kids in the morning by walking in the room and telling them, "It's time to get up, it's a bright new day with all kinds of possibilities." As you might imagine, I've had many different reactions from my children over the years.

I have three children: a daughter who is 28, a son who is 21, and my youngest daughter is 15. There is never any doubt that my oldest daughter "got it." Just about since the time she was old enough to talk she was trying to answer the telephone in our office. She would get very upset with us if we told her that she was too young to answer the phone. And there were times when people would call and there would be this little voice on the phone saying, "Bridal Expo, can I help you?" There was more than one occasion when I had to explain that my daughter had picked up the phone and no, I didn't hire children to work for me.

Anyhow, my oldest daughter always understood that every day brought new opportunities and you had to take advantage.

On the other hand, my son never really seemed to respond. I would go into his room, wake him up, and he would get up and go about his day. I never really knew whether what I was saying was sinking in and whether he understood what I was telling him. Then, when he graduated from high school, I had an opportunity to see his high school yearbook. At the high school he attended they allowed seniors to put a saying in the yearbook under their picture. And while most of the kids in the high school were saying things like, "rock on" and "high school rocks," my son had placed the saying, "Every day is a bright new day with all kinds of possibilities" under his picture. I was proud of him and I understood that he got it and it made sense to him.

My youngest daughter was about 13, when one morning I went into her room to wake her up and I said, "Sagan, get up, it's a bright new day with all kinds of possibilities." I instantly realized that I had a teenager on my hands when she rolled over, pulled the covers over her head and said, "Yes it is, and it will still be there in two hours." I understood that she got it and she really did have to wake up, but inside I was laughing so hard I had to leave the room.

My friends, every day is a bright new day with all kinds of possibilities. I understand that in recent years we've been going through economic turmoil. I understand that when we turn on the news every single day we see negativity upon negativity telling us how bad things are in the world. But I also understand that not a bit of that matters to us if we simply go out every single day and do what we're supposed to do, namely finding qualified prospects and presenting our concepts to them. We will have a good day.

The mainstream press the United States is out of control. For some reason, they believe that handing you a steady diet of negativity and bad news is somehow going to endear you to them and have you come back to them time after time after time for news. Yet exactly the opposite is happening. I understand that the Internet is taking away some of their business. Smart phones continue to provide more information in the palm of our hand than we could have had in an encyclopedia just a few short years ago, and newspapers are absolutely freaking out because their readership is dropping faster than the stock market in a depression. But the one thing these masters of the universe don't seem to understand is the newspaper stopped reporting news and for years has simply been reporting their version of the news. I was once in a situation where 300 people in our town wanted a particular measure to pass the city council. There were two people who were opposed to the measure. Yet in the newspaper they chose to give the negative viewpoint the same amount of coverage as the positive viewpoint.

If you had read the newspaper, you would've never known that there were 300 people saying yes and two people saying no. You would've thought that the town was evenly split on what they wanted to do. When I approached the newspaper reporter about this she said it's their job to present both sides of every issue; but while they did present both sides, they certainly didn't do it in a way that was accurate or fair. I believe many people are abandoning newspapers because they stopped being accurate and fair. Yes, it's true that it's easy to get your news another way and that certainly impacts their readership; but at the same time, biased, unfair reporting and the fact that they trumpet any negative thing they can, is causing people to abandon newspapers in droves.

It's no wonder that in the morning when you get up and read the newspaper you start to believe that the world is falling apart. Then you turn on the news and you see NBC, ABC, and CBS all telling you how bad things are. Before you even leave the house, you've been pounded with negativity and all you really wanted to do was have some coffee, eat some breakfast and see what was going on in the world.

Every day is a bright new day with all kinds of possibilities. I'm not telling you to abandon the newspaper and the news. I'm simply suggesting that you don't buy into the theory that the world is so screwed up that everything is negative. The mainstream media is never going to stop trumpeting negativity. So, you have a choice. You can buy into what they're saying and start every day in a bad mood or you can go to work, do the things you know need to be done to make you successful and make a lot of money for your family.

If you simply concentrate each and every day on finding prospects, qualifying the prospects, conducting presentations and closing sales, it doesn't matter what the major media outlets say; you had a good day. You put money in your pocket and you're taking care of your family. All of the talking heads on TV get paid to tell you the bad news. Their livelihood doesn't depend upon them being able to listen to their nonsense and still do their job, because their job is giving you as much negativity as they can. You need to cut through the crap, abandon the negativity and make sure that each and every day you give your family the best opportunity you can by doing the things that need to be done to close more sales. If that means you need to cancel the newspaper, not watch the news and not listen to the radio on the way to the office, so be it. I do listen to the news, I just don't let it impact me in a way that would stop me from being able to do my job effectively.

Motivation

There is an old saying that people are motivated by pleasure and pain. I believe this is completely inaccurate. In fact, I don't think people are motivated by pleasure at all. I believe that most of the people I've met in my life are motivated by fear. That's right, good old-fashioned fear. I found that people are far more likely to do something out of fear than they are to do something based on the potential for success.

We've all met people who've been afraid of failure. They will do anything to make sure that they do not fail. I've also met many people who are motivated by the fear of success. These are less likely to admit that they're afraid of success, but they are the people who seemingly sabotage a very successful business or selling situation just before the end and cause you to scratch your head and wonder why did they do that. All they had to do was follow through with A, B, or C and they would've had an unbelievable outcome. But they didn't follow through, the opportunity fell apart, and they ended up with nothing. It's a sure sign of a fear of success.

Understanding the people motivated by fear is important. It's important when you sell something, and it's important when you work with other salespeople. I'm not saying that it's bad, I just want you to understand why many times we provide a client with an opportunity or incentive that we think is a no-brainer and is going to help us close many more sales, yet when we implement the promotion we find out that not many people are interested in it. I believe this happens because people are just not motivated by pleasure, they are motivated by fear.

I will give you an example of a friend of mine who had an unbelievable opportunity for car dealers at a time when car dealerships were closing at a rate of 45 a week and yet the car dealerships he contacted were so blinded by their fears that they could not see the opportunity for pleasure in his offer.

He worked for a time with an advertising company that would contact auto dealers and provide them with an opportunity to receive leads via the Internet at no charge. Once the car dealership received the lead and closed the sale, my friend's agency would receive a small commission from the sale. He would call up car dealerships and say something like, "We want to list you on our website for free and provide you with leads of people who have logged in and said they want to buy a car from you. The only thing we want you to do is service the prospect, sell the car and provide us with the commission." There was no charge to be in this program and all of the advertising that was done upfront online was provided for the dealership absolutely free. The car dealership had absolutely no long-term commitment, no investment, and only had to provide mentions in their existing advertising and of course, the commission after the sale of a car.

My friend was amazed as he called literally thousands of car dealerships with this incredible opportunity during one of the biggest economic downturns car dealers had seen in 50 years and yet 99.5% of the dealerships he spoke with said they were not interested. He simply could not believe that the dealerships didn't understand what a good deal this was for them. And by the way, it truly was a good deal for the car dealership. After a few months of working with just a handful of car dealerships, they found they had many more customers asking for cars that they could not service and they had to shut the site down. They would have five people in Las Vegas who wanted to buy cars, but they couldn't find dealerships in Las Vegas who wanted to work with them.

He had an opportunity for car dealers and he thought it would provide them with a significant amount of pleasure. They would have to do a very small amount work yet make a large amount of sales, but for some reason the car dealers that they contacted just couldn't understand the pleasure; they were not motivated by pleasure, they were motivated by fear. I believe it was the fear of the unknown, and they simply weren't able to move past their fear and accept the potential pleasure of making more money. I'm sure there are several dealerships that my friend contacted that went on to close their doors, go out of business and cause unemployment for/of their entire staff. My friend had the perfect offer, yet no one took advantage of it.

How often does this happen to you? Have you ever made an offer to a prospect that you believe is absolutely too good to pass up, yet the prospect was not in the least bit interested and never purchased the product. Many salespeople I know try to incentivize prospects to purchase their product only to find that while the incentive they offered was very positive, it wasn't enough to close the sale.

What Is Your Job?

Think about it. Don't read forward yet; just think about what your primary job is within your organization. I've asked presidents of companies, hourly employees, and part-time contract workers. As you might imagine, I've received a wide range of answers. I've been told, "I'm the president of the company; I make everything run." I've also been told, "I'm the catering manager, and without me they wouldn't be able to have an event." In fact, I've been told just about everything you can possibly imagine at one time or another, but rarely do people get the answer to this question correct.

There's one simple job that every person in the company has. You can be the janitor or you can be the president, and you still have this one responsibility to either the owners or the stockholders. It seems many companies have lost sight of the fact that this one primary job is more important than all other. I believe that forgetting this primary job is why we have companies that are laying off thousands of people in an economic downturn. I'm amazed that some of the largest companies in the country, who profess to have unbelievable training programs and access to information that the average entrepreneur can only wish for, don't understand the basic principle that everybody has one primary job.

The job is to sell product and make money for the company. The number one job for every employee is to be a salesperson before everything else.

The next time you're interviewing job applicants, I want you to ask them one question. I don't care if they are applying to be a stock clerk, an accounting person, a human resource manager, or any position in your organization. I want you to ask them what their most important responsibility to the organization would be if you hired them.

If they don't say, "To sell product, increase profits, and create a better customer experience," don't hire them. They don't get it. There are people who seek out jobs within companies that are as far away from the sales department as possible. They say things like, "The reason I'm in accounting is I can't stand selling. I'll leave that to the Sales Department," or they say things like, "I hate high-pressure salespeople. I never want to be one." If they say that during an interview, don't hire them. If you hear this from existing employees, terminate them immediately. Show them the door and send them to the no-sales abyss they long for.

One reason virtually every government agency eventually becomes a sink hole of inefficiency is because of this type of attitude. Let's take a look at the Postal Service. Recently it announced it would lose up to $7 billion. It is in a severe budget shortfall. So how do the geniuses that run the postal service respond?

Do they increase service, extend hours, create new opportunities, and make it easier for people to use their service? No, they want to do just the opposite. Their "must do" list includes:

- Raising rates
- Cutting hours
- Closing locations
- Cutting back on service

They simply don't get it. The reason the postal service is always losing money is that it has an inferior product that's overpriced and a staff of unionized, unmotivated people who don't work efficiently. There are far too many rules regarding what management can't do, rather than rules about what employees must do. It's the same at most school districts.

How does the postal service expect more people to ship more mail if it closes offices, reduces service, and cuts hours? Only in the heads of government bureaucrats would this make sense. They have forgotten what their real job is.

Every postal service employee should be tasked with increasing profits, selling product, and creating a better consumer experience. They need to find ways to be more efficient by dropping a bunch of the union rules and making it possible for people to do more than one job, and they need to reward employees based on performance instead of automatic merit increases that reward employees for simply rolling out of bed and showing up. If they did that instead of worrying about the latest contract, they wouldn't be going bust; even with the growth of email, the postal service could thrive.

In my organization, the simplest job every person has is to sell our product. Not all of them do it in a sales presentation, but all of them realize that their primary responsibility—the one that keeps us in business—is to sell our company or concept and our service to every qualified person they meet. If our accountants aren't proud enough of our service that they will sell it, then they don't belong here.

Every person who works for your company is a salesperson also. I understand that many of them don't actively participate in conducting sales presentations each day, but virtually everyone must market and promote the organization.

The driver who delivers my dry cleaning to my front door is a salesperson for that business. Let's say there's a problem with my dry cleaning and I say to him, "Excuse me, my last order was returned and one of the shirts was still dirty." At that point, he becomes a salesperson trying to keep my business. Whether or not I continue to use his service is completely dependent upon how good a job he does solving the problem and selling me on the fact that it won't happen again. If he apologizes and fixes the problem in a professional manner, his boss is going to make money from me for years to come. If he acts disinterested or doesn't handle the problem appropriately, then chances are I'm going to stop using the service and his boss is not going to get any more of my hard-earned money.

Recently, I had an opportunity to try a different car rental organization in Denver than I normally use. My wife and I arrived in Denver, boarded the shuttle and made our way to the rental center. When we arrived we were surprised to find 30-40 people in line and about 25 people sitting around the front office. There was one person helping customers and it was obvious the line was going to take some time. I had joined the frequent renter club the car rental company offered online, so I approached the window labeled "club members." Eventually, an employee walked by (trying not to make eye contact) and I asked him, "Is this the place I should be to pick up my car?" The employee said, "You're in the right spot, but we don't have any cars. We expect about 20 cars to be returned over the next six hours and you can get in line and wait." As you might imagine, I was other than thrilled. I then said, "Are you saying you don't have cars for walk-up customers or you don't have cars for anyone? I have a confirmed reservation." At that point, the guy threw his hands up and said, "Hey, I just work here, it's not my fault people don't return their cars when they should. You can wait with everyone else or we can take you to another company!"

Thirty seconds later, I was next door at Dollar Rental picking up a car. Dollar Rental knew there was an overflow next door and jacked their rates up by 100%, but that was better than sitting around for six hours waiting to see if we could get a car. EZ Rent-A-Car will never get my business again. One employee has cost them thousands of dollars in business because they didn't train their staff how to handle a rough situation. Obviously, buying a few cars would help them as well, but I'm sure a former postal manager probably runs their company.

This is why it's so crucial to make sure that everybody in your organization first understands that his or her job is to be a salesperson. They need to respect clients and handle every situation in an appropriate manner. Someone who specifically runs away from that responsibility is somebody who's going to do a bad job when you need them to step up. You need to go through your entire staff roster and eliminate anyone who isn't going to help you make money every day.

I understand this sounds harsh, and your first reaction may be, "I don't want to terminate them, I need to train them." Frankly, my first reaction would be to try to retrain them as well. What I've learned over the years, however, is that people who are truly dedicated to not being in sales, those people who believe that sales is something they either can't do, don't want to do, or try to stay away from, cannot be trained to be professional salespeople. It's crucial to your organization that everybody is on the same page and understands that first and foremost they need to create income every day. If they're not creating income, they are dead weight and you don't need them.

I also believe that many times it's the people who aren't immediately affiliated with the sales department who can be your best bird dogs for new business. For example, when someone calls your accounting person to discuss payment on a photography package, there should be incentives for your employee to discuss additional services and create up sales. Maybe the couple bought the $3,500 photography package, but as your person is talking to them about their payment, he or she notices that they didn't purchase a frame to go along with the 24 x 36 image that they've ordered.

Many people in accounting would tell you that they don't feel comfortable suggesting additional product; after all, they are in accounting. That's wrong. Your accounting staff, your service personnel, and any employee who has contact with a customer should know that first and foremost the primary job is to make sales and profit for the company. If I had an accounting person who would not talk to the customer about additional product, I would show them the door and let them go to work for a business where sales success is not the primary goal.

Many people, including business owners I've met, are comfortable saying things like, "I stay in the background and I don't deal with the customers." Or, "I really don't like selling all that much, so I don't sell." The bottom line to advertising success is you have to be a salesperson, no matter who wants to tell you different. We are all salespeople!

Now, let's take it one step further.

"Hell, there are no rules here –
we're trying to accomplish something."
Thomas A. Edison (1847-1931)

Chapter 3 – Terms That Matter

As we've seen in the previous examples, people face a myriad of challenges. We want to equip you with the information you need to be more successful. In order to do that, we need to establish a baseline or a way for us to set a standard that you will draw from as you move forward.

Tom Hopkins, a sales champion, whose books and tapes are required items for every one of my sales representatives, taught me much of the information we discuss here. Over the years, we have taken much of Tom's basic information and adapted it to our clients' needs. I honestly can't point to any one technique that will move you from complete sales failure to complete sales success; it is a totality of the presentation that helps people achieve success. The old saying, "It's not where you started, but where you end up," is true when it comes to growing your business. We need to establish a common standard and standard terms so that we can have a significant degree of success along the way.

Definitions

I've noted in many different sales courses and in working with different sales-related businesses that each has its own terms and phraseology. In this book, we have very specific phrases that we'd like to use, and I want to be sure that as you read you have an understanding of the terms and phrases that will be used.

You can always use terms like deposit, contract, and pitch, and you will make some sales, but I firmly believe that by following a different path and using professional terminology designed to meet the client's expectations you will be more successful.

It's commonly understood that you have less than 10 seconds to make an impression when you first meet someone. The majority of the information that people perceive during those 10 seconds is visual. That's why dressing successfully plays an important role in successful selling, but no less important is successful speaking.

If people suspect that you're unprofessional or untrustworthy by the way you dress, you will confirm that perception if you don't speak well. I'm amazed at the way the sales profession has spiraled to a point where it's not uncommon for the average sales rep to dress poorly, speak poorly and not know their product. Walk into any major electronics store and you will find a steady stream of uneducated, unmotivated and under trained teenagers, who are tasked with the responsibility of showing you how to best spend thousands of dollars on a television.

It's important to use the correct verbiage as you present your product. Later in this book we discuss why people buy and a major contributor to the successful sales experience is using the proper verbiage.

Lead

A lead is any live body that may need my product. It's very simple; anyone, anywhere, who may need your product is a lead.

Contact

A contact is any live body that I contact.

Again, this may seem very simple, but a contact for the purposes of the sales professional is any live body you contact.

Appointment/Visit

An appointment is any live body I present my product to. The interesting thing about visiting with a prospect today is that while it's usually best to have visits face-to-face, you can still visit with a prospect without seeing the person. As we work towards the *Secret to Sales Success*, we're going to find that it is very important to meet face-to-face with as many prospects as we possibly can; but the definition of an appointment is anybody I present my product to. We're going to explain why we call them visits instead of appointments in a bit.

Sale

A sale has a definition a little bit different from the others. My definition of a sale is any live or dead body that pays me for my product.

I'm not picky when it comes to selling product. If somebody who's passed on wants to buy my product, I'm going to sell it. This definition is not as simple as it may sound. For many business owners who employ salespeople, there's often a debate about what the sale is. In the business owner's mind, it is clear. The business owner believes that a sale occurs when a contract or agreement is turned in with an accompanying deposit or initial investment. If both an agreement and money are not received, it's not a sale.

In contrast, many salespeople like to call a successful appointment or contract, even without an initial investment, a sale. How many times have you heard a salesperson say, "Well, I just got a great sale," and then you find out sometime later that what they really meant was, "I just had a great visit, and I think it's going to be a sale someday"? Some of the hardest working salespeople I've known have had a very hard time understanding the simple fact that it's not a sale until you have a written agreement or the client's deposit, which we call their initial investment.

Part of the *Secret to Sales Success* is to stop doing things the way you've done in the past. It's a fact that if you have not achieved the success you want over the last few years and you repeat exactly what you've been doing for the last two years, you're probably going to end up with the same results. So take a moment to not only understand the terms we're going to explain, but also think through the reason why we use that verbiage. I understand that this may be a little uncomfortable. Whatever discomfort you have now will be more than offset by the feelings of success that you're going to feel 12 months from today.

Now that you know the general definitions, you need to know some basic techniques. The way you present yourself and your business matters, but did you know the very words you use can make or break a sale? Here are some additional terms that we use in our business that we have adopted after learning sales techniques taught by *Tom Hopkins*.

Buy vs. Own

People have a much harder time buying something than they do owning something. When you own something, you typically are willing to invest more in it.

Contract vs. Agreement

I believe that when you are working with a customer, whether you call them clients, customers, or another name, there is an awkward moment when you pull out the contract. As you'll learn later, when it's time for your office to secure an agreement with the customer, it's an easier transition and less formal when you don't call the paperwork a contract.

Sign vs. Approve

In order for your clients to invest in your service and own it, they need to approve the "paperwork." It's much less threatening than asking them to sign "the contract."

Pitch vs. Presentation

We never pitch our product. In fact, I hate the word "pitch" when it comes to sales. As a professional salesperson, I believe it cheapens what I do when it's called a pitch. And that's not what salespeople do anyhow. "Presentations" allow you to work with potential clients, discover what their needs are, and ensure that you have an opportunity to fill that need.

Professional presentations should be conducted with a track to run on. When I see a sales professional talking to a client without using a brochure or some type of information to guide their presentation, I know that, in most cases, that presentation isn't going to include all of the necessary information. A simple brochure, organized in such a way as to present the best features of your product, is the easiest way for you to be sure that each and every prospect receives the same information.

Deposits vs. Initial Investment

We also do not take deposits. That doesn't mean that we don't require our clients to provide us with a form of payment when they secure services. We do in fact require every new client to make an initial investment for the services they requested. I'll admit, some of this seems like word games and, in some cases, it can become ridiculous as to what word you use or don't use. However, in the case of the word "deposit," that's not the case. As a sales professional works with the prospect, the latter wants to know that the sales professional is going to help them create the service, product, or result that they expect. And I believe every sales professional truly wants to help the prospect do just that. Much of what we do as sales professionals is perception before it is reality, and we want the prospect to have the perception that the product they receive is going to be exactly the way they have always envisioned it. It's the sales professional's job to make that dream a reality.

I know that every sale is going to have minor unscheduled challenges, but the competent sales professional will handle last-minute issues and problems in a way that the client never sees, ensuring that the product they sold performs the way it should and is delivered as promised. If you're working in an organization that routinely under delivers or over promises, it's time you seriously consider finding a new company to sell for; or better yet, maybe it's time to start a competitive organization that can deliver on its promises.

It's important that from the very first time you start working with the prospect you stay on point and stay on message that you're helping them receive what they want. To that end, many prospects have some resistance to placing a deposit on a dream. However, that same prospect won't have any concern about making an "initial investment" to ensure their dream comes true. That's why we always require an initial investment from our clients. We are forming a bond with them to ensure the success of whatever they're investing in.

Appointment vs. Visit

Don't you enjoy a visit more than you do an appointment? I always think of appointments as rigid, set periods that frankly don't sound very fun. You have an appointment with your dentist or doctor. You have an appointment with your attorney or accountant. You visit with your friends. Don't be put off by the fact that a visit seems more casual. You can still achieve a significant amount of sales success by having a track to run on when you visit with the prospect.

"Evil has no boundaries and the righteous have no balls."
Chris Evans – Author (1957 –   )

Chapter 4 – The Truth About Knowledge

Knowledge Is Not Power

We've often heard that knowledge is power. As a professional sales person, you need to have knowledge; and if you believe what many nationally known authors and seminar instructors teach, you will believe that the more knowledge you have, the more power you have. As if knowledge alone will move you from the unknown, unsuccessful sales person to a sales leader in your industry.

Many years ago, I had an opportunity to attend a sales training seminar for the insurance business. Insurance salespeople from all over the country descended on San Jose, California to attend a one-day training where several of the industry leaders would be speaking. On the stage, there were eight of the insurance industry's top salespeople. Many were names you would immediately recognize, and everyone in attendance was excited to hear what pearls of wisdom they would offer.

Throughout the day, one after the other would stand at the dais and tell the thousands of salespeople in the audience their best advice on how to sell more insurance. The salespeople in attendance were furiously taking notes, trying to capture every word the speaker uttered. Finally, late in the day, the most known speaker, the God of insurance, rose to speak; after speaking for about 45 minutes, he wrapped up his prepared comments and took questions from the audience. One after another, people came forward and asked this all-knowing guru their question, until finally one guy in the audience asked him this question. He asked, "You're the best known and best paid insurance agent in the country and today you're standing here telling all of us your secrets and showing us how to cut into your business. Why would you do that?"

The gentleman on stage smiled and said, "First, I want you to know that's probably the best question I've ever been asked at this type of event." He went on to say, "What I know, that you don't, is that while all of you today are sitting here listening to what we say and writing notes so you can remember it tomorrow, there is little if any chance that any of you are going to return to your office tomorrow and do it." The audience was shocked, but I immediately understood what he meant.

Even after sitting through an all-day seminar and taking page after page of notes, the average sale professional in the room was going to return to their office the next day and do exactly what they had always done. There was little chance that anyone would take the knowledge this industry leader shared and apply it to their everyday activity. They would return home, go to the office and repeat the same unsuccessful practices that they had always done since learning their bad habits early in their selling career.

There was no chance that anyone who listened to him speak would compete against him because they only had half the formula; and while we are all told knowledge is power, the truth is knowledge by itself is just knowledge and knowledge by itself can't do anything. You have to add one thing to knowledge; to make it useful, you have to add implementation. If you don't apply the knowledge, nothing will happen.

What the speaker understood was that most sales professionals loved knowing "how" to do something, they were just a lot less likely to actually apply the knowledge.

Knowledge + Implementation = Power

How to Lose Weight

Take a look at weight loss. The weight loss industry in the United States generates billions of dollars in sales every year. Millions of people spend hard-earned money on the latest fad so they can lose weight, yet who among us doesn't inherently know the formula for losing weight? Losing weight is a simple three-step process:

1. Eat Less.
2. Exercise More.
3. Repeat.

It doesn't take $500 and the latest book on the chocolate diet to reduce the amount you weigh; yet there are people who have struggled with their weight their entire life. I understand it's a struggle and I'm truly not trying to make light of it, but knowing how to lose weight isn't that hard. We all have the knowledge. What most of us are lacking in is the implementation.

Losing weight today is hard. Implementing a balance diet is something that's way easier to suggest than do. We all have active lives and need to eat throughout our day, and many times the food options available to us are limited and not all that healthy. But that doesn't change the point that knowledge of how to lose weight isn't the issue; it's the implementation of that knowledge where people fail.

As sales professionals, you attend seminars, buy books and study techniques to acquire knowledge, but I want to encourage you to implement what you learn. I have a proven technique that I teach to wedding professionals. I have a book out titled *How to Double Your Wedding Business in 12 Months*. I show wedding professionals exactly how to double their business. I have hundreds of testimonial videos on my web site from people who have used my system to acquire more clients. There's no doubt that my system works. Yet when I stand in front of a group of people at a Bridal Business Boot Camp, I know that less than 10% will actually implement the very program they are excited about at the training. I always know which 10% implement the system because they are the ones writing emails, phoning and sending testimonial videos. They are easy to spot. They are the people with larger checking accounts.

You must implement the knowledge you acquire or you're just a knowledgeable failure.

"Diplomacy is the art of saying 'nice doggie'
until you can find a rock."
Will Rogers – Actor (1979 – 1935)

Chapter 5 – A Secret

I want you to concentrate and remember what I've written. All authors do. We want you to read our books, remember what you have read and implement the techniques we try to teach. To that end, most books you read will try to put information into a format you can easily remember. Authors try to create something so simple that if you don't remember anything else, you will remember that. I've never been a real fan of doing things with crayons; but what the heck, let's give it a try.

I want to share with you a way to remember the key elements of my sales system. In fact, I want to tell you "A Secret." This is The *Secret to Sales Success*, so a Secret is appropriate.

The way to remember the steps to the perfect sales system is to remember "A Secret."

A = Automation
S = Use a System
E = Education
C = Consistency
R = Repetition
E = Experiment
T = Track Your Work

Catchy, wouldn't you say? Seriously, it's easier to remember things when you have a simple way to take complex ideas and remember them. That's why your mother and father taught you the ABC song. It was easy to remember because you both sang it and memorized it. In our case, you don't need to sing, just remember that you know a secret!

Before we start talking about "A Secret," I want to explain to you my BIG SECRET and why I believe the vast majority of books written about selling are a waste of time and money. You see, I've spent thousands of dollars on sales books over the years. If it's in print, chances are I've purchased it. I've spent countless hours studying what others have to say about selling, and I've come to one conclusion. Most authors of how-to-sell books know very little about how to sell.

I'm not sure if they have just forgotten what it was like to sell products every day or if they truly could sell the way they teach in their books 200 years ago when they were salespeople, but the majority of what I read either won't work today (probably didn't work then either) or isn't effective.

I'm also continually amazed at how each person has a hard luck story that leads them to a moment of discovery and then a calling from on high to spread the word to the rest of the world. The stories typically go something like this:

- I was a crappy salesperson.
- My boss was a crappy boss.
- I was broke, lonely and tired.
- I was just about ready to quit when,
- I went on a discovery mission.
- I captured all the information I could.
- I scoured the world for hidden data.
- I discovered something everyone else missed.
- I felt a need to tell the world!
- Now I'm the world's most in demand sales trainer!
- You can be rich like me.

Ok, maybe I'm exaggerating a little, but you have all seen the format and you know I'm right.

Here's the problem with 98% of what I've read about selling over the past 30+ years.

They make it way too hard. Selling isn't hard. Selling comes down to a couple of simple principles that can be used by smart, educated people, on a consistent basis, over and over again in a strategy that's open to new ideas. It's not hard.

Think of yourself as water. I like water. In fact, I drink it all the time. My favorite is Fiji water. I believe it's the best water I've ever had but that's not why I like water. I like water because it always finds the path of least resistance.

No need to slam up against an obstacle when you can go around and reach the same conclusion. Water instinctively knows how to get the job done with as little effort as possible. I think one of the things that will make you tremendously successful is to sell like your water.

You don't need 20 closes and 15 different presentations f you have on or two that are effective. That's why I think most books on selling are nonsense. The authors make it way to hard. It's as if they have to convince you that their book is worth $25 so they load it up with 150 pages of nonsense and then give you the real idea in the last 100 pages. As I said earlier, I want you to receive value from the information I'm sharing no matter how long it takes, but quicker is always better than slower.

Let's be water. Let's explore the Secrets of Sales Success keeping in mind that we want to implement them in the easiest way possible.

Evans Truism Number Three

The amount of money I put in my checking account is directly related to the number of sales I make.

A SECRET

A = Automation

In the Webster dictionary, automation is described as the technique of making an apparatus, a process, or a system operate automatically. Most times, I believe the average sales professional misses the importance of automation in the sales process. Earlier in this book, I spoke about why sales is not a numbers game, but that doesn't mean that you don't need a steady supply of quality prospects to talk to. Automation, especially in today's Internet-based world, is one sure way to keep your sales system up and humming along, but it takes some knowledge, implementation, and planning.

Occasionally, I'll speak before a group of people at a convention or workshop, and when I come to the part about automation someone in the audience will raise their hand and ask, "Don't you think that our prospects and clients expect one-on-one personal attention?" I understand where the question comes from.

Most sales are still a one-on-one (not necessarily face-to-face) proposition where one person conveys an idea, system, or product to another person and a mutually beneficial opportunity is struck between the two. I believe the interaction between two or more people in personal relationships is still important and will continue to be, but automation used properly in no way impedes the mutual relationship developed between a sales professional and their customer. It actually enhances that relationship because it provides both with more time to focus on the need the prospect or client has.

It's also important to note that the vast majority of automation you will use as a sales professional is designed to generate prospects and complete tasks that you are better off handing to someone else. If an individual who makes $12 an hour can handle writing a Blog about your product, it's not cost effective for you, a sales professional averaging $100 an hour, to write the Blog. Those types of tasks can be delegated to individuals and organizations that are probably better at it, enjoy it more and will complete it faster than you can. After all, if it took one hour for a great posting on your Blog, it would cost $100 for you to do it and $12 for someone else to do it; and when you have someone else do the task, you are free to do what you do best – sell. It breaks down like this:

A) 1 hour at $12 for a staff member to write a Blog post = $12 cost to you

B) 1 hour at $100 for you to write Blog post = $100 + 1 hour lost production $100 – Total loss $200

This doesn't address the fact that you should have made progress towards a sale during the one hour you were selling, so the actual cost to post an article on your Blog could be several thousand dollars! It's simply more cost effective to let automation help you reach your sales goals. That's why I have listed it as the first step in the *Secret to Sales Success*.

I live in California. Or as our former philandering, over-the-hill movie star governor liked to call it, Cal-Ee-For-ne-ah. No matter how you pronounce it, there's no denying that California has some of the most unfriendly business practices in the country. Few businesses in their right minds choose California for a place to headquarter their business. With Nevada, Arizona, Utah, and Oregon close by, most businesses look at California and run.

The rules and fees placed on employers with staff in California are ridiculous. It's no wonder that so many organizations are looking for ways to outsource their staff and have work done in other locations.

I'm not talking about outsourcing work to India or the Philippines. With a US unemployment rate of over 9%, you don't have to look very far to find many people willing to take on tasks and complete work for you. When those people are in a different state or can be hired as independent contractors, there is a value to outsourcing your administrative tasks.

Now, let me say for the record. I'm not an attorney or accountant. I've never even played one on television; so if you have legal or accounting questions about my advice, you will need to talk to a professional. Don't take this advice as gospel because:

- The rules are always changing.
- Each situation is different.
- I'm not an Attorney or Accountant.

Now that I've done the proper legal notice, let's get back to my point.

Businesses across the country are taking a look at the cost associated with having an in-house staff and are realizing that there are substantial savings if they can get away from the idea that everyone needs to be in one place to get the job done. One hundred years ago, when you needed your entire staff in one place because that was the only way to effectively communicate, this model made sense. But now we are in a new age!

It appears that Al Gore has finished inventing the Internet and now the rest of us can live off the benefit of his hard work. We don't need to be all in one place to get the job done. Yet the average sales organization format is still the same as it was before smart phones, iPads, and the Internet. It's just like an industrial factory from 1920. You hire a person and you entice them with good pay and benefits. One of the main reasons you hire one new employee over the other applicants is you believe they can do the job and you think they are going to be an asset to your team.

Then you give them an office or desk and a computer, and you chain them to it from 8 am to 5 pm Monday to Friday. If they don't come in one day or don't answer their cell phone by the third ring, you start to wonder what they are doing and if they are working. Then you look out and see your staff of 10 sitting around talking and you wonder why they aren't working. You don't want to be rude, so you decide to start having weekly or daily meetings where you outline the projects for the week, so you can clearly define what needs to be done. You're confident that just a little supervision is what's needed.

Now regular staff meetings are part of your daily life, and before long you notice that everyone attends the meetings and then goes back to exactly what they were doing before the meeting, so you're forced to kick it up a notch and the meetings become a lot less fun and more like mini bitch sessions; but hey, you're the one paying the bills and you need the people on your team to perform because things are getting tight. At some point, you decide the entire team needs to attend a training session to pull together as a team, but after a weekend of sitting in circles, holding hands, and chanting or trying to learn how to be a trapeze artist, things seem to be about the same.

Before long, you start thinking that you can't figure out how the great people you hired became a babbling mass of incompetents. You feel like you have to babysit the staff to get anything done and nobody understands how important it is to get some work done.

From the staff's perspective, they can't figure out why the boss who seemed super cool when they first started working has become the Napoleon of the sales world. There are a ton more rules and the company that once seemed so fun has become all work.

Then the state steps in and tells you that as an employer you have to pay twenty-five different types of taxes because you have employees. Then there's the insurance costs, overhead costs, training costs and before you know it your life becomes a series of sessions of you sitting up at 3 am trying to figure out what the heck has happened and how to fix it. Your beautiful sales business that you once enjoyed so much has become a monster that's going to eat you alive.

The problem is the business model. It's just like going to a used car lot and buying an old car. Sure, you can get it on the freeway and it runs fairly well, but all the other cars are faster, more reliable, more fuel-efficient and they don't break down as often. To be sure, they do break down sometimes; but when a new car breaks down, the parts are always readily available to get them running again fast! As my good friend Bill Bokelmann found out recently, you rarely find yourself standing by the side of the road, halfway between Las Vegas and Phoenix, on a 105-degree summer day in a new car.

Before I beat this point to death, I want to make one more observation about in-house staff and outsourcing or automating your staffing needs, and I'm going to include myself in this observation.

It seems to me that when you get five or more good people together in one room, they become completely ineffective. Great people, smart people, people who are sharp. Take good people, put them on a committee or board and it's as if you stripped them of their brains and they became idiots. It's no wonder Congress sucks. I sat on the local City Council for several years, as well as our local School Board. I'm glad that it was more than 10 years ago, because today I would be coming across the table and choking half the people involved in the process. Forget the fact that 50% of the people who came before us to speak had no idea what they were speaking about. We collectively would sit and discuss things until 1 am and never reach a conclusion, so we would have to come back and do it all over again. Congress recently did this with the National Debt Limit. Months of arguing only to "kick the can" down the road until after the next election. It's a symptom of a broken system. In any event, put people together on a committee and you have a babbling mass of incoherent nonsense; and then, if you speak with one of them, they will tell you how hard they work. George Bush used to say all the time, "It's hard," or "We're working hard," as if the American people had expected him to become president and take a four-year vacation. Of course it takes hard work. You're the leader of the free world! It takes work.

Let's face it. Particularly in the sales profession, most of us don't work hard. We all go to a place where we meet other people. We sit around and do something that we are expected to do until it's time to go home. Then we tell our spouse and family that we were at work, working hard, when in fact we were simply hanging out at a location with a bunch of other people who wanted to look like they were working hard also. Thank God 5 pm rolled around because you were running out of ways to look busy. Most of us don't do hard work. In fact, I'll bet most of us work at less than 30% capacity.

Understanding that the vast majority of people don't work anywhere near their capacity offers you, as a sales professional, significant opportunity. You don't have to go out tomorrow and work at 110% just to get ahead. The truth is, if everyone else is working at 30%, you can move in front of them by working at 31% capacity. Kick that up to 50% capacity and you're a Rock Star! Automation can make you a rock star.

Automation can help you work smarter, work more, save you money, save you time and allow you to focus on the areas of your business where you excel. Hopefully, that's selling. Let's take a look at four areas of automation and some of the services that can help you with automation. The areas are:

- Staff Automation
- Lead Automation

- Follow Up Automation
- Really Cool Automation

Staff Automation

There are two services I use for staff automation. I'm sure there are others, but these two have been able to provide me with all the assistance I have ever needed and one in particular is my "go to" service. Those services are:

www.Elance.com

I have found that Elance has one of the biggest networks around. You will find providers from all over the world and the price ranges for tasks can be from dirty cheap to professionally expensive. Over time, I have used them about 170 times and even found a full-time assistant through this service. I have gotten tasks like articles, market research, brochure design, advertising design, script writing, editing, logos, graphic design, and some web design consulting through Elance. Also, Elance goes well beyond just Internet marketing tasks. The process is very simple and you are not obligated to choose anyone if you don't find a provider you're comfortable with.

www.Odesk.com

Odesk allows employers ("buyers") to create online work teams coordinated and paid through the company's proprietary software and website. The name is a short version of "no desk," in reference to the company's intent to enable anyone to work anywhere, anytime. I have primarily used Odesk for computer software development and customer service tasks.

It's important to understand that there are specific guidelines you need to follow in order to have a successful relationship with a remote contractor.

Be specific in your task. Don't list a job as "design a brochure." You need to be as specific as you can be, for example:

"Design a 8.5 x 11 tri-fold brochure with postage paid reply card that meets the artwork submission guides of XYZ printer. The brochure will have full bleed images throughout which I will provide. I will provide the copy. You will have to contact the US Postal Service for the postage paid indicia. This is four color, both sides and is intended to generate a desire by the reader to pick up the phone and call us. We like a techno look and are not afraid to try something different. We will make a special offer on the reply card. The job begins when I assign the work and must be completed and delivered within 5 working days."

When you are specific in your needs, you will find providers will post bids faster, for a lower price, and the end result will be better.

Always check the providers' references. Both services allow you to see samples of a provider's prior work, and they allow past customers to rate the provider. If you only want 5-star providers who have done over 100 jobs online, you simply enter that into your request profile and that's who will receive the information. You should also look at their portfolio and decide if it's real or just a sample. Sometimes, particularly with design services, a provider will post templates, not work they have actually produced. Feel free to question providers before you assign the task.

Use the web site escrow service. Elance in particular offers you an opportunity to post any money for the provider in escrow and then release the funds upon successful completion of the work. It's a win-win for everyone. The provider knows the money is available because you placed it in escrow. You know you're going to receive the final work before the provider receives the funds. The escrow service simply keeps everyone honest and above board.

In 2005, I almost lost $1,350 using www.Guru.com. Their escrow didn't work the same way I described above and a young lady in Texas took my money and didn't deliver any product. Unfortunately, Guru had delivered the money to her, so I was left with no other choice but to charge back my credit card. When I charged back the credit card, a representative from Guru called and said it was a violation of their rules and I needed to wait for them to resolve the issue. They gave me an option. Leave the money with them until they figured out how to get it back or lose my membership in Guru and be banned for life. I'll miss them.

In my opinion, the two services listed above have better escrow features and offer better protection. In fact, I once made a mistake and accidentally paid a provider based in India, $2410. instead of $24.10. I quickly learned two things.

- There are honest people all over the world.
- Elance has an excellent backup system

The provider corrected my mistake and returned the money before I had to contact Elance, but had I needed it, Elance old me they could have resolved the issue for me and recovered my funds.

If were your provider is based is important to you, be sure to watch where providers come from. Today, many Americans don't want to outsource work to other countries, so they shy away from services like Elance and Odesk. The truth is it's easy to limit your job offer to specific regions and even states if that's what you want to do. I follow a few simple rules that you may find helpful too/as well. I don't have an issue using foreign contractors per se, because the money I save using them is simply reinvested in my business locally.

- Never use India or Philippines for customer telephone contact.
- Every provider must have a significant track record.
- Every provider must have references.
- When dealing with foreign nationals, be specific.
- Always set milestones to follow.
- Always rate your providers so others know your experience.
- If they claim to be US based yet have a thick Indian accent, they are lying.

To my last point I want to add that many of the foreign providers have caught on to the fact that US based businesses are sensitive to outsourcing work overseas. They have registered their company on the services and listed a US based address as an office. I've found that, most of the time, it's a PO Box they use to appear as if they are US based. I'm not saying you won't receive great service and I use services from India, Pakistan, Hungary, Canada, New Zealand, and Australia all the time. But if only working with US based providers is important to you, you will need to be careful and be aware.

I've also used wonderful services from Mississippi, Virginia, California, Nevada, Arizona, and many more. It's truly a fact of life that we live in a world that is flatter every day. It's not uncommon for me to get on Skype early every morning and again late every night and discuss a project with a provider in India, Pakistan, or England. Then, later in the day, I'll talk with Australia, Canada, or Columbia (excellent telephone skills). It's amazing how interconnected we are in today's world; and as you become more automated, you are going to find that your reach throughout the world will be significant.

My assistant Amy is a wonderful young lady. We talk several times a day. She pays all my sub-contractors and handles all of my travel arrangements, speaking engagements and virtually everything an admin assistant sitting next to me in Malibu would do. She just happens to be in Florida and we have never met. I hired her through Elance.com and she has been a valuable asset since day one. Thanks, to Skype, cell phones and email, we're in constant communication.

In fact, the book your reading has been edited and proof read by a service provider in Romania. I received several bids to review this book prior to sending it to the publisher and the fact of the matter is the qualifications and ability to turn the product around quickly were why I selected Anna P. There were other services less expensive (some US based) but another thing to always remember is you get what you pay for.

Lead Automation

Lead automation is an area where most businesses believe they have set up a great system, but when you take a closer look you find the vast majority of lead generation systems don't work. Obviously, there are some systems that are better than others and we want to concentrate our time and effort on the best systems. So while this review will touch on every lead generation system you'll find, I'm going to concentrate on the systems and services that work best.

Interestingly enough, many businesses have a webpage, and because on the webpage they have a place for people to register they wrongly believe that they have an effective lead generation system. By far, the vast majority of businesses I've worked with who have lead generation on their webpage don't effectively use that data to generate sales.

Typically, it goes something like this. The leads are generated somewhere within the system and eventually wind up on the sales manager's desk. Then, the sales manager at some point in time transfers that lead to a sales professional. Once the sales professional receives a lead, it sits on his desk for a while and then, eventually, he may follow up. It's not uncommon for a lead to take 30 to 60 days in larger organizations to get to the sales representative. This is simply far too long and a complete waste of time if that's how your company is currently treating leads that are generated from outside sources.

The wonderful thing about automating your lead system is that you have the ability to direct the lead to the proper person immediately. And you even have the ability to follow up on that lead even before it's assigned to a specific sales representative.

Let's face it, we live in a world where everybody expects something to happen immediately. I distinctly remember when the fax machine first came out. It was a revolution in business because it gave businesses the ability to transfer contracts and paperwork and receive signatures in minutes, not days. Then e-mail came along and now we have the ability to transfer information in seconds not minutes. However, this has caused what I believe is an unrealistic expectation by customers and business associates that everything can be handled within the next 10 minutes.

The smart sales professional doesn't try to buck the trend and put barriers in the way of their potential customers. I'm always amazed when I send an e-mail to a business and I receive back some type of e-mail that asks me to input information and prove that I'm a human so that my e-mail be delivered to the recipient. There are many services available on the web that are designed to eliminate the spam in your e-mail box and provide you with only e-mails generated by people you want to talk to; but I'm always amazed at the businesses that use spam blockers without thinking about how many potential customers they're actually blocking from reaching them.

A general rule of thumb I like to use is if your e-mail begins with, "I'm sorry to send this to you," it's probably not an e-mail you want to send to prospective clients. And since when did spam become such a problem? Nobody receives more e-mails than me, I average somewhere between 900 and 1,200 e-mails each and every single day. I video to establish filters that screen out about

95% of all the spam and I never once make it hard for my customers to reach me.

The important thing about automating your lead generation is to be sure that the lead was quickly and efficiently routed to the place it needs to be for the fastest follow-up.

There are two services I use for the automation. Both of these services offer both lead automation and follow-up automation; and because I always try to concentrate on services that don't require a huge investment, I believe that both these organizations are very cost-effective.

Aweber.com

AWeber is an online service that provides you with the ability to do several things, including e-mail newsletters, sign up forms, manage your subscribers, create auto responders, and HTML e-mail templates. AWeber, in short, is a full service e-mail handling service that you can integrate into your lead program quickly and efficiently and have it up and running in just a few short minutes.

I like AWeber because it's cost-effective and provides me with the ability to have someone register on my website and then immediately be transferred into my online database. Even before I respond to the prospect, AWeber provides me with the ability to send the prospect information and put them into a newsletter rotation system that keeps my company name in front of them continually.

For example, if you register on my webpage today, you will receive an e-mail back saying thank you for registering and the first copy of my business newsletter. Now even if I'm not in town and I can't personally follow up on that lead, you will receive a welcome e-mail in the first newsletter. But let's assume I'm out for a month and I'm not going to see that you registered until I get back. AWeber allows me to program in dates for you to receive the second and third newsletter. So if you register for newsletter today, you will automatically receive newsletter number two in 10 days and newsletter number three 10 days after that. It's completely automatic and doesn't require constant supervision to be effective, yet it affords me the opportunity to effectively deliver my message to prospects at all times.

The second service I want to talk about follows the largest e-mail delivery service on the Internet, but they may also be the most finicky e-mail service on the Internet.

ConstantContact.com

ConstantContact.com is the granddaddy of e-mail delivery services on the Internet. They've been around longer and have more clients than anyone else. Unfortunately, they're also one of the most expensive services on the Internet, and they have some very strict guidelines that you must follow, or your account will be shut down.

What most people don't understand about constant contact is that they have a very strict list of domain words that they will not e-mail to. So, even though they profess a 94% delivery rate, you have to remove every e-mail in your database that starts with for example info. If you have an e-mail address that starts with info@, Constant Contact will not deliver e-mail to that address.

Many of the businesses I work with have a client database with thousands of e-mails and inevitably, out of those thousands of e-mails, several hundred will start with info@. That means if that business uses Constant Contact to deliver their e-mail, none of those clients and prospects will be receiving the e-mail.

Constant Contact publishes a list of 23 key phrases that they do not e-mail to. You need to be sure to cross-reference that list against your mailing list before you use Constant Contact. Also, Constant Contact has the strictest interpretation of the anti-spam laws. They routinely shut down accounts other services allow.

That's not to say that Constant Contact is a bad service, They have stricter rules than many of the other service providers and, if you're going to use them, you need to be aware of the rules.

Follow-up Automation

Both of the services listed above also offer the opportunity for follow-up. It only makes sense to integrate both your lead generation and follow-up automation if at all possible. It's important to have an organized follow-up system paragraph and, I believe, the majority of sales leads are not called upon properly or promptly.

I understand that's not startling news, but the fact of the matter is if you're generating 10 leads a week and you only follow up on having him, you'll be losing 50% of your business every single year. I don't believe that the average sales professional doesn't follow up on a lead because they're lazy. I believe they don't follow up on the lead because they're disorganized and they don't have a system to follow up.

With a very small investment and a little bit of planning, you can have a stellar lead generation system.

Additional lead generation and follow-up sources

Swiftpage – www.swiftpage.com
Vertical Response – www.verticalresponse.com
iContact – http://go.icontact.com
Mail Chimp – www.mailchimp.com

S = Smart – Think Smart / Be Smart

It's simple, you have to have a consistent plan, you have to be smart about it in order to be a sales professional. Part of being smart enough to be a professional salesperson is being organized enough to be a professional salesperson. By far, the biggest problem I see in most sales organizations is a lack of planning, not a lack of smart people being available to create the plan.

I want you to be smart and only entertain those systems and processes that are going to allow you to move your business forward. Part of being smart is understanding **what** is and is not good for a sales professional.

Gone are the days when the average sales professional would go for a three-martini lunch, then to dinner and have seven Bourbons, chase women all night long and go to work the next day and make sales.

Today, more than ever, there needs to be a balance in both your business and personal life. As a sales professional, it's important to understand that there are basic requirements of the job that you need to master. Fortunately, no one aspect is that hard to master, but when we put them all together it becomes a significant challenge. The basics that I believe are important for every sales professional are:

- Prospecting
- Contacting people
- Qualifying
- Presenting your product
- Listening to their concerns
- Closing the sale
- Asking them for help and referrals
- If you structure your business to follow the smart formula, there may never be a time when you won't have a ready supply of prospects and customers in these.

E = Education

Continuing your education throughout your selling career is important. If you're working with an organization that doesn't want to provide you with the resources to have ongoing education, you will have two options.

You can find a new organization to work for you so you can invest in your own education. The reason education is so important is it provides you not only with information but also a frame of reference for what's going on in your business today. More and more laws are being drawn, upward professionals have to have continuing education in order to keep their licenses. Getting the sales profession has no such requirement.

You can hang your shingle as a sales rep with absolutely no training, and unfortunately many people do. It may seem a little strange talking about continuing education to somebody who purchased a book to educate themselves, but I encourage you to keep investing and educating yourself so you're always current on the latest techniques.

Let's face it, many of the presentation techniques and closing styles that were useful in the 30s are still useful today. But frankly, very few people have created anything new; still it is important to have ongoing education because you learn the new systems and services that are available to help you sell more products. It's just as if you try to sell using the first phone that Alexander Graham Bell ever invented; you certainly can make some calls, but it wouldn't be as effective and as efficient as it could be. One thing you need to be in today's business environment is efficient.

I also believe one of the great benefits of ongoing education is that it levels some of the highs and lows we tend to experience as sales professionals. Only a sales professional can understand what I say when I talk about the unbelievable high of closing a particularly tough sale and the unbelievable low of losing a sale that you thought was a sure thing. By having ongoing consistent education, I believe you keep your mind in the right place to face any challenges that may come your way.

Additional online resources for ongoing education:

Evans Sales Solutions – www.evanssalessolutions.com
Dale Carnegie – www.dalecarnegie.com
The Sales Board – www.thesalesboard.com
Tom Hopkins – www.tomhopkins.com
Tony Robbins – www.tonyrobbins.com

C = Consistency

A sales rep can be working for one company one day and for a completely separate company the next day. I have a friend who for many years has averaged about three selling jobs a year. And every time she joins a new organization she is convinced that organization is the best company on the planet and nobody can do what they do. Within about 90 days, I receive a phone call and she will tell me all about the problems with the company she's working for and ask if I know anyplace else that she might be able to work. Consistency is not one of her strong suits.

But I'm not just talking about consistency as staying with one company and working through good times and bad, I'm talking about the consistency of your work ethic each and every single day.

Today, we often hear that having a routine or structure to your day is something bad. The modern man doesn't do the same thing over and over again as our fathers did in their careers. As if it's bad to find a job, happily work in a job for 35 years and then retire. It seems that in order to be successful by today's standards you have to be non-conventional and avoid a routine at any cost.

The sales professional has to have a routine. It has to be a routine that includes some very good basic selling skills. I want to encourage you to look at your calendar and plan ways that you can be consistent. Ways that you can have time every day to educate yourself, time when you can prospect, and time when you can be with your family.

One of the key characteristics that separate mediocrity from excellence is consistency. Not very glamorous I know, but it is absolutely 100% true.

Being consistent in *purposeful* actions is so critical, and yet can be so very challenging for creative sales professionals who have lots of ideas and *stuff* that they want to accomplish. I know it has certainly been a challenge for me at different times, both personally and professionally.

Many times, consistency gets confused with *routine*, which sounds boring and totally uninspiring. Blah! Nothing, in fact, could be further from the truth. Consistency simply means taking the actions that bring you closer to your desired goals. You definitely need repetition, but it doesn't need to be boring!

And…that leads us to where most of us get tripped up: we set ourselves up to fail in two ways:

How many times have you said, "Well I did really great this week, but next week I'll probably mess up"?
Or,
"I did ok this time, but I probably won't be able to keep with it"?
And you know what?…That is not your fault. Your experiences, personality, thoughts, beliefs, and the cumulative mix that makes you YOU have all conspired to sabotage you; but the good news is that you can change it.

The fact is that when you start thinking of yourself differently…you start to do things differently. Think of yourself as a successful sales professional and, the fact is, you will be a successful sales professional.

The other main reason we trip up is *that we don't give it enough time to work.* In this "Age of Instant," if we don't get immediate results…we think it doesn't work. It's imperative that you set aside a proper time and place for it to work.

Here are some ideas to help you with consistency.

- Batch stuff – group items together (do your writing tasks at once, group your phone calls together, handle your email and correspondence at one time, etc.).
- Keep a time log. You'll be amazed at where your time is going and how you're spending it. Track ALL of your activities: what you do, how long it takes you, and so on.
- Make a schedule. I know, I know it seems to fly in the face of being a creative, dynamic entrepreneur, but you need a plan. Planning out your activities will provide you with a structure to achieve consistency.
- Chunk it. If you have tasks you tend to put off, make a commitment of 10-15 minutes to devote your attention to it…that is certainly doable (set a timer if need be).

Consistency is one of the keys to sales success!

Additional resources for planning and consistency:

Zoho Planner – http://planner.zoho.com
Keep and Share – www.keepandshare.com
The Daily Planner – www.thedailyplanner.com
Microsoft Office 360 – www.microsoft.com/en-us/office365

R = Repetition of Advertising and Promotion

We've all heard that saying:

As a sales professional, you have to have consistent repletion to be successful. I was once working with a sales professional who sold professional services. His goal, as with most sales professionals, was to sell more product, which had been a problem for a few years as sales were flat. Additionally, profit margins were being squeezed and using his income dropped. He tried numerous ways of reaching new prospects and customers, from direct mail and postcards to television advertising. However, none of these methods had much of an effect. His sales remained fairly flat and even began to decrease, as he was finding very few new customers.

We took a look at his marketing plan, and his goal was to spend around 3% of his revenues on advertising. He said he didn't really have a marketing or advertising plan per se, but he was looking for that one advertising medium that would produce the best results. One challenge I recognized immediately was that he was very impatient and didn't seem to want to invest the time that it would take the lead in the advertising plan to develop. He appeared to be switching from one form of advertising to another, looking for that one that would bring in many new customers or the magic bullet.

It's perfectly reasonable to expect results of advertising dollars; however, it takes repetition of the marketing message to get a potential customer to act from your advertisement. We all have busy multitasking lives, and we are bombarded with information every day. It's not uncommon for your clients to have information overload, and there's certainly no indication that we're going to be hit with less advertising messages in the future, so it will only get worse. Trying to balance this against the requirement that customers typically don't act on an advertisement unless it's both unique and repetitive can be a challenge.

The National Chamber of Commerce recently put out a study which shows that customers see your advertising 5 to 7 times before they respond. Potential customers need to be frequently reminded about your firm and products. If you take a look at companies like Nike and how they put their swoosh symbol everywhere and associate athletic venues, you'll understand how important it is for the client to see consistently your message in order to respond.

Repetition and unique advertising generates a top-of-mind awareness. It's this awareness that brings new customers. If I'm an insurance agent, I will want my company's name to be the very first one that a potential new customer thinks out. That way, they'll contact me when they need service. And the only way to accomplish this top-of-the-mind awareness is through repetition of advertising in many different forms of media.

While you should always have a consistent professionally designed message that you're trying to relate, repetition of that advertising message is usually far more important than the message itself. As a professional sales rep, it's very important that you promote your message everywhere your potential customer may be so that when the time comes for them to make a buying decision you're the first company they think of.

Additional resources to help the advertising message reach out.

PRWeb.com – www.prweb.com
Bureau of Labor Statistics – www.bls.gov/oco/ocos020.htm
Google Ads – http://www.google.com/intl/ln/ads/
Cardlytics – www.cardlytics.com

E = Experimentation

We all have a tendency to find something that works and then use it for so long that it becomes ineffective. Imagine if today you were using a promotional technique which was popular in the 80s. Would it be as effective or as useful as it was back then?

Specifically, I remember faxing information to people. In nearly 80s, it was perfectly acceptable to have a mailing list of a thousand people and then fax some information about your product or service. Then, over time, people decided they didn't like the fact that they were receiving unsolicited faxes, and eventually the practice was banned. If you were to still use that technique today, not only would you be breaking the law but also it would be very ineffective.

That's why it's important not only to use what works but also to experiment with new techniques at the same time. I'm by nature fairly curious when it comes to what services are available and what things I can incorporate into my business to help me be more efficient and reach more people. I tend to spend a certain part of everyday looking on the web to find new services and programs that are applicable for my business situation.

Not every service I come across is effective or useful. In fact, many of the services I find, particularly on the Internet, are completely useless. But just because I find a few services I can't use doesn't mean that I'm going to stop looking. Today's professional sales reps have to be willing to experiment with new services, programs, and techniques.

There is a saying that if you're not moving forward, you're moving backward. This is particularly true in the sales profession. One way that you can incorporate successful experimentation in your business is to change the mindset of how you look at experimenting with new services. There's much to be gained by learning from failure; and in a company culture, you may recast the entire notion of failure by creating a culture of experimentation.

Wal-Mart, Capital One, and General Electric have all implemented a culture of experimentation into their organizations, and they now challenge their employees to learn from their failures and find new ways to do things. As a sales professional, you need to experiment with new processes and new procedures all the time.

One area that every business seems to be experiment with these days is social networking. In my boot camps, I have a slide that says, "Social networking is crack to a desperate world." You can't turn on the TV, radio, or read a newspaper without somebody talking about the importance of social networking.

One thing I think we have forgotten in the discussion about social networking is that it's not the networking that it's important, it's the result. To that end, we've created an entire marketing campaign that says, "Fans are great, customers are better." In other words, what's it matter to spend 15 hours a day on Facebook if you can't convert them into real customers.

Everyone sees the experimenting and trying all of the new services that they hope will bring them leads and customers, but the truth is most of the services won't generate any more leads than you yourself can generate by getting out and meeting people. It's important to experiment with new services, but it's just as important to remember that as you experiment you're simply trying to generate more customers, you're not creating a new lifestyle.

I had a friend who purchased a Corvette. Now I have to tell you that it was a very nice Corvette. It had all the options you could think of, it was fast and you could tell by his attitude when he drove it that it made him feel very special to drive the Corvette. It wasn't long after he purchased the car that he had a leather jacket with the Corvette logo on it. Soon after that, he had some coasters in his house with the Corvette logo, and that was soon followed by posters in his garage, wall hangings of the Corvette logo, welcome mats in the front of his house with the Corvette, and slowly, but surely, his entire house became a Corvette museum. He crossed the line from driving a car and using it as a utility vehicle to making the car a statement on who he was. I didn't quite understand it, but then again it made him happy and who cares if he wanted to become the King of Corvettes.

I notice quite a bit of the same thing happening with people when they start their social marketing campaigns. They join Facebook and start to learn what Facebook is all about, and before you know it everything they do in their business is online. From the moment they wake up in the morning to the last thing they do before they go to bed at night, they are tweeting or twittering as if the entire world has to know their every movement and emotion throughout the day.

Experimentation with new things is important, but it's also just as important to remember that this too shall pass. You can't become so invested in any one thing that it becomes the only thing you do. And virtually every service you're using today will be different five years from today. As I write this book, it looks like it's very possible that Facebook and Google may take over the world, but then again we've been there before with other companies and it simply hasn't happened.

Look back at the 1940s and you'll see that the largest homebuilder in the United States after World War II was Sears. They were the largest retailer in the world, and they provided more homes than any other builder in the country. They were widely regarded as the most unstoppable company on the planet.

Move forward just a few years and think about the computer. When the computer first came out, IBM was the world leader in computer mainframes. They were widely regarded as unstoppable and unchallengeable when it came to computer electronics. Companies trying to do business again somewhere couldn't survive that because there were such large organizations that they could step on competition without even thinking about it. It seemed the entire world believed that IBM would be a world leader forever.

Now, in 2011, it looks like Facebook, Google, Apple, and Yahoo are all businesses that can't be stopped. I'm certainly not suggesting that we should look for ways to stop them; in fact, I respect their size and the great products that most of them deliver. My point is that while today they may look like they are unstoppable and unchallengeable, in just a few years from now there'll be somebody new who's going to look unstoppable. You can't become so invested in one thing that you let it become a lifestyle instead of a service that you use. I love Apple computers and I use them whenever I can, but that's where it ends. They provide a service which I find effective, and as long as they do that I'll continue to use them. When they no longer are able to provide the service I need at the price I can afford, I will find someone else.

That's why it's important to experiment at all times with new services to help you sell. The following websites offer some great opportunities to help you grow your you sales and be open to new ideas.

Additional Education Resources

The Deal – www.thedeal.com
Chief Executive.net – www.chiefexecutive.net
Inc Magazine – www.inc.com
Freakonomics – www.freakonomics.com

T = Tracking

As a professional sales representative, it's important that you have an organized system to track your progress. Over the years, I've met many sales professionals whose only tracking system was either in their mind or on a scattered group of papers somewhere on their desk. To achieve professional results, you have to have a professional process with which you can track prospects and sales.

Most business tracking can easily be defined as the procedures companies follow to track their overhead as well as the return on investment. The importance of implementing anchored business tracking applications is self-evident to any business that is trying to succeed in an unstable economy.

The past few years have had a severe wake-up call to sales professionals and businesses alike, as they work to improve their business situation. There's little debate that you need to be able to track both your expenses and your opportunities as you move toward sales success. The adage that "it takes money to make money" is only beneficial if the company or sales professional does in fact have money to invest in a down economy. An organized tracking system will allow you to know exactly what your options are both in good times and in tight times.

Because of the current economic climate, sales professionals have a leg up on larger corporations. While some may argue that larger corporations have more resources to draw from and can last out a bad economy longer, an argument can be made that because an independent professional salesperson doesn't have the overhead and systems and thus have to go to make changes they have the ability to make adjustments more quickly and thereby benefit from the efficiency of being small.

Spending money to make money isn't a bad thing when you have the money to spend; but when the economy slumps and sales are down, most sales professionals start looking at every penny that they can to cut an expense. As a sales professional, things are more directly under your control. You don't even send out a memo to 500 people telling them to use less packing material. Because of this, you control the speed with which you can implement changes in your system, and your ideal position is to keep overhead low and create a better and more immediate return on your investment.

Tracking software is a great way to understand how your business is doing, what your expenses are, and what changes need to be made in order to keep you profitable. It's important to note that in a bad economy little details that may not have mattered a couple years ago can now be the difference in a profitable business, or just making ends meet.

Quite often, people will comment on my obsession to track as much data as possible relating to my business. We track everything from the number of telephone calls made to us, e-mails received by us, e-mails sent out by us, inquiries on our website, and many more metrics that provide us with a solid picture of what's going on at *Evanssalessolutions.com*. On any given day, we can tell you exactly how many people visit our website and how many of them purchased product. We know the conversion rate, the average sales rate, and any one of 100 other small pieces of information we capture.

The importance of capturing the information is not just to take it and let it sit in a file. We routinely take the information out, look at it and analyze what's going on in our business so that we can be more profitable. Today, there are literally hundreds of websites that can help you track what's happening in your business. The sales professionals have a much wider range of services available to them now than they've ever had before. The great news is, many of the services that are available to sales reps imply virtually no cost or for very small investment.

One of the services we like the best and we use on a regular basis is Zoho.com. Zoho allows us to have a database of clients that can be shared with anyone else in the world. Having multiple employees spread out across multiple countries, it was tough for us to find a database and fill all of our needs. Zoho allows us to have people in any country have access to the data, and when they see it it's the most current up-to-date data we have; no need to wait for a daily update or some information to change. If one of our staff members in Florida finds one the phone numbers incorrect, the minute they change it in our database everyone who has access to that database will have the correct information.

One of the things I particularly appreciate about Zoho is that it's completely customizable and completely scalable, which means if one month we have five employees, and the next month we have 25 employees, we can scale the database and purchase extra seats for very reasonable investment. As I write this, I believe the most expensive options Zoho offers is $25 a month per user.

Over the years, I found that many sales professionals don't track their success for two reasons. Number one, it's monotonous. And number two, it's expensive. While I understand that tracking your clients, prospects, and sales is not the most thrilling thing you'll do every single day, it's a necessary part of your business; and you will find that once you start tracking as many aspects of your business as you possibly can, your business will grow and you'll be able make smarter decisions quicker because you have more information available at your fingertips.

Additional Tracking Resources

ReferralKey – www.referalkey.com
SalesForce – www.salesforce.com
BNI International – www.bni.com

Evans Truism Number Four
The number of presentations you perform is directly related to the number of face-to-face visits you set.

CHAPTER 6 – The Perfect Presentation

Here we are, the moment we have been working for, the moment when we visit with the prospect face-to-face and receive their order. This is your opportunity to learn about the prospect and what their goal is for your product. You can find out what their needs are and start formulating a plan to fill those needs.

Most sales professionals understand the need to take time with the prospect to find out what they want. We have all heard the saying, "God gave us one mouth and two ears so that we could listen twice as much as we talk." We've all heard it; few try to abide by it. In recent years, it's become fashionable to talk about the presentation being an educational opportunity, and various speakers are touring the country giving seminars about the need to "educate" the prospect and then close them. I certainly don't want to take away from their good work, but my experience has been that some prospects are just too hard to educate! I want to close them, not send them to college.

I do have a formula that I like to use when I'm conducting a presentation. It's simply a process I have developed that allows me to present my information in an orderly way and that leads me to the best possible opportunity to close the sales. First, let me ask you a question:

What Is the Primary Purpose of the Presentation?

If you are like most of the sales professionals who attend my seminars, you will answer like this:

To tell about your product.
To learn about what the prospect wants.
To explain features of your service.
To find out the prospect's budget.
To build a relationship with the prospect.
To answer their questions.

It's true that all of the things listed above are important, but they are not the purpose of the presentation. They are simply a part of the presentation. The presentation offers you an opportunity to tell the prospect about your product, but that's not the purpose of the presentation. Think of it this way. You are not meeting with the prospect to:

Tell them about your product.
Learn what they want.
Explain features of your service.
Find their budget.
Build a relationship.
Answer questions.

Why are you meeting with the prospect?

Just as all your advertising should focus on scheduling face-to-face visits, all of your presentations should focus on closing the sale. Everything in the presentation should be geared toward closing the sale. The goal of the presentation should not be to tell the prospect about your product; but as you tell the prospect about your product, you should be doing so in such a way as to make it easier for you to close the sale.

Many sales professionals would say, "I met face-to-face with Diane and had a great time. We talked for an hour, and I really think she's going to buy with us. I gave her all my information, and she was excited!"

Obviously, Diane wasn't that excited—she didn't have to commit to using your service! If the purpose of the presentation was to educate Diane or learn what Diane wanted, then I guess it was a success; but if the purpose of visiting with her face-to-face was to have her give you the initial investment on your fee, you failed! I believe the purpose of the presentation and every salesperson's job can be summed up in three words:

Close the Sale

Just as your presentation should have a track to run on and an end goal of closing the sale, it's important to understand that there are some important emotional triggers that every prospect has. In fact, all of us have them when we are considering a purchase; and many times, these emotional triggers are far more important than the price of the product we are looking at or the practicality of owning it.

I have a friend who owns a cake shop. Without a doubt, he is one of the best bakers in California. As with most business owners, my friend spends many hours each day running the store. It's not unusual for him to be at the shop at 8 a.m. and not go home until 9 p.m. On weekends, he's working all day Saturday; but occasionally, he will go through an entire Sunday without stopping by the shop. He works a lot.

About two years ago, he was driving by the Long Beach Convention Center on a Sunday and noticed it was having a boat show. Being spontaneous and thinking it would be fun, he decided to stop in. His wife thought it would be fun as well, so off to the boat show they went.

Three days later, my friend, who's never sailed a day in his life, was the proud owner of a 30-foot sailboat. It seems he decided while walking through the boat show that he was spending too much time at the shop. His solution was to store a significant amount of money in the form of a sailboat in a marina. Somehow, he felt that if he spent a bunch of money on a boat, he would take time off work and use it.

When he told me the story about buying the boat, I asked him, "What made you invest $30,000 into a sailboat?" His answer was simple; he said, "I just wanted it. The more I spoke with the sales rep, the more I wanted it; and before I knew it, they started calling me captain."

My friend ultimately did use the boat quite a bit and sailing has become a fun outlet for his entire family. Seems his theory worked, and he did start taking time off. However, let's look at what happened when he met with the boat salesman. The boat salesman understood the reason for the presentation. Everything he did during the presentation was designed to close the sale by doing one thing: create desire!

What Is Desire?

Have you ever seen a child, about 4 years old, who really wants something? They get excited and jump up and down. They squeal and yell, because they want it so bad they can't control themselves. If the child is that excited about getting a candy bar, how hard is it for the mom to get the child to eat it?

Obviously, it's not hard at all. The mother has to do nothing more than give the child a nod, and the candy bar is gone. No need for five power closes or a 30-minute interview to discover her wants and needs. It's like handing raw meat to a pack of wolves. The candy is gone before you know it.

When's the last time a prospect felt that way about your service? Do prospects get excited? Do they want to call all their friends and tell them about the great service or product they just booked? If your clients are not excited when they book your service, why not?

What about the prospect that keeps asking questions for three hours, and then, almost reluctantly, decides to use your service. Why did it take so long, and why are they not excited?

Let's take a look at my good friends at the Walt Disney Company. One of the many things I admire about the Walt Disney Company is that everything it does, it does well. If it's not done well, you never hear about it. I was once on a tour of MGM Studios in Florida, just before it opened to the public. The tour guide was taking us through some of the buildings and describing the reason for being decorated the way they were.

At one point, she said, "And the green you see on this wall is Mr. Eisner's favorite color. In fact, we originally painted it blue, but he changed it." We were surprised. Here, the CEO of a company the size of Walt Disney was involved in the selection of paint colors for a public area of MGM Florida. At first, I thought it was a little strange, but the more I thought about it, I realized that Michael Eisner had a vision of how that area should combine with the rest of the park to create excitement and help people have a great experience. If people have a great experience, they will be more likely to come back to MGM again. The wall color was a small part of creating a mood and, thereby, a desire to visit again.

If your prospects aren't excited at your presentation, they won't have enough desire for your service. It's also true (and very cool) that when a prospect is excited and does have desire, he or she will always invest in your service.

Sometimes, sales professionals try to create desire the easy way. They think that by offering their service at some drop-dead price they will entice every prospect to use them. However, my experience has shown that while prospects do consider price, they also want to have the product fill their need. They will adjust the budget when there is enough desire.

Look at it this way: Do we buy what we need, or do we buy what we want? Even now, when the economy is suffering through a very tough time, most people don't walk into the thrift store and ask for the least expensive shirt. People still buy what they want, and what determines their degree of "want" is desire.

During your presentation, you will help the prospect build desire for your service. Desire leads to want, and we all know what the prospect wants, the prospect gets.

How to Create Desire

There is a very easy system that I have taught thousands of people over the years that's going to help you build desire. This is simply a formula that I want you to use at every single presentation you perform. Sales professionals have used this system over and over again, and thankfully, because most people have a tendency to react to similar situations in similar ways, it's successful more often than not.

Nothing is going to work 100 percent of the time. Many of the presentation skills we are going to discuss work well, but they will only move the desire meter a nudge, not a mile. If you have an overpriced, poorly implemented product that the prospect can clearly see isn't worth the investment, your ability to create desire is going to be ineffective. For the sake of our discussion, I'm also going to assume the following:

- You believe you have the decision maker at the visit.
- You are in an area that's conducive to visiting with the prospect.
- You're not trying to do nine things at once.
- Your cell phone is off.
- You have a brochure and a track to run on.
- Your product is professional.
- You're dressed appropriately.

If you can say yes to everything listed above, then we can move on; but before we do, I must take one minute to talk about cell phones. Just as the prospect won't wait in line to meet you at a trade show, they won't sit there while you answer 20 "important" calls.

Asking them to look through pictures while you fight with a prospect from six months ago about the balance on their account isn't going to create much desire—except the desire to escape.

Most cell phones have voice mail and, believe it or not, every text you receive doesn't have to be answered within 30 seconds. The cell phone used to be a useful tool. It's quickly becoming a huge time waster.

Fabulous Features

Think about it this way: You have two new cars that look identical in every way. They are sitting on a car lot, side by side. As you look over the cars, you find that the one on the right has tons of features and the one on the left has nothing.

The car on the right has power steering, power brakes, electric windows, a GPS, and satellite radio. It has reclining seats, heated seats, an adjustable headrest, and cruise control. To top it off, it has a top-of-the-line built-in security system.

The one on the left doesn't have any of that. It has roll-up windows and cloth seats. It does have brakes, but that's about it. From the outside, they are identical. Now, answer these questions:

Which one do you want? Which one will you enjoy more? Which car do you feel better about driving? Which car fits you better?

If you are like most people, you will want the car on the right. The car with all the features seems like a much better car. Even when the car on the right costs more than the one on the left, most people would want it. How do we know? Car manufacturers sell far more cars loaded with features than stripped-down cars with no features.

The car on the left is new, runs fine, and will get you where you want to go, but the dealership will sell 10 cars loaded with features for everyone that they sell that's stripped down.

People don't buy what they need; they buy what they want. How do we make them want? By giving them features!

What Is a Feature?

I've attended many seminars where the leader has spent tremendous amounts of time trying to define what a feature is. Usually, the speaker introduces some detailed chart that walks you through a process, and you ultimately arrive at a list of features.

I'm going to give you a slightly easier way to identify features. I believe a feature is anything about your product that you think is cool or you're proud of. If you're a carpet cleaner, it can be the quality of your equipment or the way you dress when working. Maybe it's the package you put together or the speed with which you clean carpets. A feature can be the fact that you have an AAA rating with the Better Business Bureau. Even though we've recently found out that it looks like the Better Business Bureau will give you a higher ranking if you join them and a lower one if you don't, some of the public still perceives the Better Business Bureau as a good thing.

You are the best person to decide what you feel is very cool about your service, so make a list of the top 10 features of your product.

1. _____

2. _____

3. _____

4. _____

5. _____

6. _____

7. _____

8. _____

9. _____

10. _____

Why 10 features? It's simple. I only want you to think about half of what you're ultimately going to need. That's right. Eventually, you are going to need to develop and memorize a list of 20 features of your product or service.

Now that you have developed a list of 10 features, I want you to take some time and create a description of each one. During my seminars, I find that people tend to say things like, "We're a full-service photographer." While I understand what that means because I have been in the business for many years, I promise, the prospect doesn't have a clue about what that means. The most important part of having a list of features is being able to explain them in such a way that the prospect understands.

Sometimes, it seems a little silly because the feature may be something like, "We smell good." (The smell good plumber.) OK, so you smell good. Now, explain it. That means you must explain how you smell good and why that's important. Why do you have to explain it? It's simple.

Have you ever had a time when you have said something to someone and they have nodded their head indicating they understood? Then, at some point later, you find out that they had no clue as to what you were talking about? This usually happens with children and employees. They look you right in the eye and agree; and then later, they do something exactly the way you asked them not to. When you ask them why they didn't do it the way you asked, they say, "Sorry, I didn't know that's the way you wanted it."

That's why you must name the feature and then describe or explain it—but we're not done yet. There is one more thing we have to do. We must tell the prospect how it applies to her and explain the benefit.

We all have a little voice in the back of our heads asking, "So what?" When people tell us something, our little voice quickly determines if it applies to or affects us, and then helps us decide on our level of interest. When we hear things that we don't understand, our interest level is low; but when we hear about something that we do understand and why it applies to us, our interest meter goes even higher. The greater the interest, the more we want the feature.

There is a very easy way to share the benefit for a feature in a way the prospect will understand. There are two magic words that help you along the way. They are "...so that...."

Let me show you how it works.

The Feature:

Our Wiffle-snapper 1000 is the fastest toaster available today.

Describe It:

Our Wiffle-snapper 1000 completely cooks your toast to a golden brown in just 18 seconds.

The Benefit:

So that you never have to wait around for some golden brown delicious toast.

You have a Feature – Description – Benefit.

Having done seminars for many years, I understand that you have to say things so people understand them. When you put F.D.B. together, it's pronounced fudub. That's not good for people to remember; so many years ago, I changed it to Feature – Advantage – Benefit, which is pronounced Fab and is much easier to remember.

When we talk about Fab-ing prospects, I really want you to fudub them, but you get the point.

Let's F.A.B.

Now it's time to take the 10 features we listed earlier and create the descriptions of those features.

1._____
2._____
3._____
4._____
5._____
6._____
7._____
8._____
9._____
10._____

The last step is to create the benefits description for each feature. Begin each line with "So that...."

1. So that_____
2. So that_____
3. So that_____
4, So that_____
5. So that_____
6. So that_____
7. So that_____

8. So that_____

9. So that_____

10. So that_____

You should now have a complete list of features, advantages, and benefits for 10 really great features of your product or service. Ultimately, you are going to need more; but for now, we're good to go.

With your prospect in place, your cell phone off, and your features ready to go, it's time to start the presentation. There is an easy formula I follow during presentations, and while it's never exactly the same, it goes something like this:

5-minute introduction
35 minutes to learn about their vision
15 minutes to ask questions and present features to cover concerns
5 minutes to wrap up the paperwork

In reality, I'm closing the sale every minute of the presentation. When the prospect says they hate something, I'm going to assure them we don't do that. When they love it, we will make sure it happens. Once they have a chance to explain their vision, I present them with the features I believe will most accurately give them the service they have dreamed of. In the vast majority of cases, the presentation is over and done within one hour.

I love the Fab-ing part of the presentation best. That's the point where the prospect starts to see how the features you're explaining have the ability to provide them with the benefit they desire. I have a list of about eight features that I start with and use to build desire. If you're not providing features that excite prospects, it's time to get new features.

There is also a very easy way to check with the prospect to make sure they understand what you have said and to provide you with feedback as to how significant the prospect believes certain features are.

How Does That Sound?

I simply explain a feature, advantage, and benefit and then ask, "How does that sound?" After talking with the prospect and building rapport for the better part of 40 minutes, I promise, they're going to tell you how that sounds.

At some point, the prospect is going to say, "This all sounds great!" At this point, you're going to forget about the rest of the features and close the sale. It's useless to keep telling the prospect about 10 more features after they have said it sounds great. What more do you need? Shut up and close the sale!

Let's assume they say, "That doesn't sound good," or, "I don't like that." It's the perfect opportunity to say, "We've had a couple of prospects feel the same way as you do. How can we adjust this to be exactly what you want?" The minute the prospect starts helping you fill their needs, you are working together with a common mission!

How does that sound? It's great, isn't it?

"When people ask me if I have any spare change,
I tell them I have it at home in my spare wallet…"
Nick Arnette – Comedian

<u>CHAPTER 7 – Closing the Sale</u>

Before I give you some powerful closings, I want to spend some
time exploring some of the attitudes of sales professionals when
it comes to closing the sale. I believe there is a huge difference
between helping a prospect-to-be make a decision that is good for
them and leading a prospect into a decision that is bad for them.

For some reason, many sales professionals appear to believe that
selling a prospect and, specifically, closing a sale is a bad thing.
That explains why so many sales professionals are so good at
what they do, but so bad at closing the sale. You must ask the
prospect to buy your product. If you don't attempt a close, you're
cheating the prospect. After all, when a prospect selects your
service, they are going to get the best possible product you can
offer, aren't they? And you are going to help them have the best
possible product, aren't you? Well, then, it simply makes sense
that you cannot be afraid to ask the prospect to take advantage of
the opportunity you offer. If every prospect who came through
your door were a best friend, would you let them make decisions
that are bad for their business? Of course not! Help yourself by
helping the prospect and be sure to give every prospect several
opportunities to take advantage of your service. You must close
the sale.

When Is the Best Time to Close the Sale?

As I've discussed this question with sales professionals, I've
received a wide range of answers. Everything from, "I give every

prospect one hour, and if they haven't bought, I let them go," to "I'm not comfortable being pushy with a prospect, so I give them the information and let them decide later."

Unfortunately, many sales professionals seem to think it's a good thing if you are not a great closer. I don't understand it, but I meet people all the time who tell me, "I don't push the prospect to buy. I hate pushy sales people." Please don't mistake the pushy people who have tried to sell you things in the past with professional sales people. Their job title may have been salesperson, but if they beat you with a rubber hose or twisted your arm, they were not professional sales people; they were hacks.

The best time to close the sale is when you see the prospect is ready. When you see the prospect is:

- Excited and talking about your service.
- Asking questions about how things work.
- When things slow down after moving along well.
- When you believe you have filled their needs and they're receptive.

There are many times to close the sale. Don't get locked into a set presentation and miss the buying signals. When a prospect is excited, invested, and interested, it's time to close the sale. Imagine you're visiting with a prospect, and they say, "This is perfect. It's exactly what I want." You now have two options:

1. You can keep talking and miss an opportunity.
2. You can say, "Well, I'm glad you feel that way, let me complete some information on the paperwork, and we will be on our way to helping you with the WiffelSnapper 1000."

The prospect may say, "Hold on. I'm not ready to place the order yet." In that case, you're going to say, "Mary, I find it easier to keep track of everything and organize my thoughts on the paperwork. That way, I won't forget anything." Then simply move on to the next feature or close. It's truly not a big deal, and I haven't ever heard of a prospect who said, "This looks good..." while getting up and running out the door when the sales professional attempted to close the sale.

Next, I want to discuss something all professional salespersons master, or they are not selling for very long. It's a technique that all of us should use more often, but because we try to control every situation, we don't. It's something that's very easy to do physically, but, sometimes, it's a mental challenge. Learning how to do this one thing well will help you close many more sales.

Successful Silence

That's right. Successful silence is the ability to say to a prospect, "Mary, I'm so happy you're excited about my service! What's the best time for us to deliver it on Thursday, 9 a.m. or 10:30?" and then shutting your mouth.

Just sit there, nodding your head, with a smile on your face, waiting for the prospect to respond. In sales, it's often said that the first one who talks after the close is set is the buyer. That means, if you set the close and then talk first, you've just bought your own product, and that's not a good thing.

You must master the art of not talking. Just sit, smile, and know that the first one who talks is the buyer.

The Assumed Close

This is most likely the close that most sales professionals use 95 percent of the time. Unfortunately, it only works about 50 percent of the time. The assumed close is simply when you find everything moving forward in a positive way. At some point, the prospect stops saying "if" and starts saying "when." It can be 10 minutes into the presentation or 90 minutes, but you will know when it's right. Simply start filling in the paperwork. Eventually, you will complete it and ask them to initial it. When they do that, you have a sale.

The most important part of using the assumed close is knowing when it's not working and it's time to move on to another technique. I've watched many sales professionals blow through the entire presentation, feeling like they were spiritual matches for the prospect, only to find out the prospect wasn't that interested.

The easiest way to wrap up the assumed close is to say something like, "Diane, what's the best time to deliver the cake, 9:00 a.m. or 10:30?" When Dianne says, "9:30 is much better," simply say, "Great, just initial the paperwork, and I'll have our driver deliver the cake of your dreams at 9:30."

When she initials the paperwork and gives you the initial investment, you're done. Next sale please!

The "I Want to Think About It" Close

Have you ever had a prospect say to you, "I want to think about it?" From this point forward, you're going to smile and know you're just a few minutes away from securing the order every time you hear a prospect say, "I want to think about it."

The prospect says something like, "Wow, John, your service is great. Give me some time to think about it, and I'll get back to you." Or statements like:

- "We discuss everything before we decide."
- "Let us think it over."
- "I need to sleep on it."
- "Can I call you tomorrow?"
- "We never make decisions on the first appointment."

- "I have to discuss it with a partner."

What the prospect expects you to say is, "That's fine. Let me follow up in a few days." Many sales professionals have a tendency to say just that, but you've already invested time in getting to know the prospect, so you are not going to let them get away that easy. Obviously, you can't be rude, but you can't let them stop the sale by saying, "I want to think about it."

In your experience, what is it that the prospect wants to think about? Is it that prospects don't trust you, or they don't think you can perform as promised? Usually not, I've found that the vast majority of the time what the prospect wants to "think about" is money. It's not always the money, but I'm sure that 95 percent of the time it is. At this point in the close, you can know two things:

1. The prospect doesn't have enough desire. They're not jumping up and down and selling themselves.

2. They probably want to think about the money, but maybe not. Many sales professionals would say something to the prospect like, "Well, Diane, what do you want to think about?" Then Diane will come up with some lame dodge designed to get her out the door as fast as possible. You simply can't be that aggressive if you are going to be a good closer. You need to be subtle, polite, and have your new friend help you out.

Understand, the vast majority of the time, the "I Want to Think About It" Close simply sets you up for the Reduction to the Ridiculous. That's because we know the majority of the time, the prospect wants to think about the money. However, you just can't let them know that you know that yet.

Here's how it works: The prospect says, "I want to think about it."

You say, "Dianne, that's great. I certainly appreciate you taking the time to visit with me today."

At this point, she thinks she's off the hook, but you're just getting started. You go on, "And I know after having had a chance to get to know you that you are going to give this some serious thought, aren't you?"

She shakes her head and says yes, thinking it over, but you continue on, "Diane, before you go, I would like to ask you to do me a favor. Will you help me understand exactly what it is that you want to think over? Is it the fact that..."

Now, notice—this is important—do not stop after the words "think over." If you stop there, you are dead. I've written it as a continuous sentence for a reason. If you stop at, "...what is it that you want to think over," you are giving her permission to answer. But we don't want an answer yet.

By continuing on with, "Is it the fact that..." you now have a chance to start into your best features again, so have your best three features ready.

"Is it the fact that you don't think our cakes taste good?" Of course, she will say no. Then you say, "Is it the fact that you don't think we can deliver as promised?" Again, she will say no.

You can keep this up forever, but I suggest you bring up two or three of your best features—things you noticed she loved during the presentation. Finally, after she has said no a few times say, "Well, Diane, could it be the investment?"

Let's diagram it:

"Is it the fact that you don't think we can deliver as promised?" No.

"Is it that you're not sure our product will fit?" No.

"Is it something about the design you're unsure of?" No.

"Well, Diane, could it be the investment?" (Here, you stop talking.)

If it is the money, the vast majority of the time the prospect will say yes. Smile, you're almost there.

What if Diane says, "No, it's not the investment"? What do you say to her then? In a loving and compassionate manner, it's okay to smile and ask, "What is it?" More often than not, the prospect is going to tell you what it is, and you say, "Thank you for sharing that. I know we can take care of that by...." And you fix her issue.

Then start closing all over again.

The Reduction to the Ridiculous

It's ridiculous how many ways you can use the reduction to the ridiculous. Simply put, the Reduction to the Ridiculous breaks whatever amount of money is concerning the prospect down so far that the amount seems ridiculous. If you've ever seen an ad in the newspaper that says the new HD television is $3,400 or $89 per month, that's the Reduction to the Ridiculous. $3,400 is a bunch, but I can afford $89 a month, even if it is for 66 months. Does the Reduction to the Ridiculous work? You bet it does, and you need to have it in your closing arsenal.

It's important that when the prospect says to you, "Your product costs too much," or "That's higher than I wanted to go," you take a moment and clarify how much "too much" is. You see, as salespeople, we tend to look at the overall number, but the prospect certainly didn't expect you to provide your product or service for free. So your $3,000 package may be more than they intended to invest, but it's not $3,000 too much.

Simply say, "Diane, I understand what you're saying. Today cost is certainly a concern for almost everything. Can you tell me about how much too much you feel it is?"

If Diane says she's seen similar packages for $2,500, the challenge isn't $3,000; it's now a much more manageable $500. That's what you focus on now, the smaller amount. Forget about the entire price at this point; focus on showing her the value she receives for the $500.

You say, "Diane, if I understand you correctly, we are really talking about $500, aren't we?"

She says, "Yes, you're $500 too much."

At this point, I like to do a quick recap of two or three of my product's features we've discussed that I know are unique to me. I don't really give the prospect a chance to speak yet, but I do want her to start seeing some of the features I have that my competitors don't.

Now you need to put it into the correct perspective. You can say, "Diane, let's work through this a little. How long will you be using our Wipple-Snapper 1000?"

She answers, "We hope to have it for 10 years." You say, "OK, 10 years is about 3,650 days, right?" She says, "I guess."

"Diane, I was just trying to figure it out, because it seems to me if we spread that $500 over the next 3,675 days, we are really only talking about an investment of a fraction of a penny each day?" She says, "I guess so."

"Diane, let me ask you one more thing. Won't the Wipple-Snapper 1000 package we've designed offer you all of the quality and expertise you said you needed from a stomping machine? And having worked with you for a while, I can sense that this package really does offer the things you want for your business, doesn't it?"

She says, "Yes, I think it will."

You say, "Great, we've agreed, haven't we? By the way, when is the best time to schedule your delivery, next Tuesday or Wednesday?"

The "No" Close

I love the "No" Close. I love it for the sheer audacity and boldness of the close. You have to be confident and sincere to use this close. Frankly, when I was first taught the "No" Close, I thought it was nonsense. I didn't think I would ever use it. Then I heard about Dennis Holt.

Dennis owned a company named Western Media. His company was founded on the theory that if an advertising agency gets a discount with radio and television stations, because they represent 10 clients, what type of discount would he get if he represented 10 advertising agencies. Over many years, he built Western Media into the largest advertising-buying service in the world. However, Dennis wasn't always the big guy on the block. In the beginning, he had to call on agency owners and fight for every bit of business. After all, there is a certain prestige to working with the network media outlets; and if the agencies went through Western, they feared losing some of the prestige.

Dennis called on one potential client who happened to be a major player in the advertising business. As they sat down to visit, the potential client started telling Dennis everything that was wrong with his concept. He went on for over 30 minutes, telling Dennis he was stupid and the idea was stupid. He used very profane language until the guy worked himself into such a frenzy that he ordered Dennis, who hadn't said three words, out of his office. On his way out the door, Dennis stopped, turned around, and said, "OK, I understand. I'm going to put you down as a firm maybe."

The guy he was meeting with screamed at him to get the hell out and Dennis left. A few years later, Dennis received a phone call from the same guy who asked if Western International would buy media for them. What I love about that story is, in the face of all the bad things being thrown at him, Dennis kept his cool and knew that eventually this gentleman would work with him.

You have done the presentation. You have explained the features. You have tried the Assumed Close, the "I Want to Think About It" Close, and The Reduction to the Ridiculous. In fact, you have tried everything—even creating closes on the spot, because you want this sale and it's just not happening. The prospect continues to say no.

Understand, at this point, you don't have much to lose. It's not like three minutes after leaving you they're going to decide they were wrong. Take a breath, put on your most caring attitude, and have some fun. Launch the "No" Close.

Here's what you say: Let's assume your wedding planner.

"Diane, I appreciate the time you have taken here today to visit with me. I have enjoyed getting to know you, and frankly, I appreciate the opportunity to build a friendship with you. I think I understand what you want your wedding to be; and if I'm not mistaken, we have created a wedding photography package that fills every one of your needs. So I'm a little concerned that having been together this long and working together as we have, if you select any other photography service, you won't receive exactly what you want. I never let my friends make a mistake when I can prevent it. So, Diane, I have to say I can't accept your no. I can't risk you not having the perfect wedding photography I know I can deliver. Diane, it can't be a no, it has to be yes!"

Stop Talking – Sit – Smile – Enjoy

I know. It sounds strange, but believe me, once you have a chance to try it, it's amazing how about 25 percent of the time you save the sale. You must be strong. You must be sincere. And remember, there isn't a thing wrong with helping a prospect decide to do business with you. You are going to give them the best possible product and service, and when they deal with you, you will know they are getting the best. Don't be afraid. Close with gusto.

One last resource I want to remind you about is *Tom Hopkins'* book, *How to Master the Art of Selling*. Tom's book will provide you with 16 great closes, as well as fantastic information that will make you into a sales champion. I have used Tom's selling techniques for years, and I have been able to have a lifestyle and career that is better than I thought possible. Purchasing *How to Master the Art of Selling* will be a great investment. After all, it's the second best book about selling I know of.

"Committee: A group of men who keep minutes
and waste hours."
Milton Berle - Entertainer (1908 – 2002

Chapter 8 - Fans Are Great – Clients Are Better

Social Networking Tips

Are you or your organization considering setting up a profile on a social networking site? Are you wondering what tasks are involved, how much time it will take, and how you might streamline your efforts? Maybe your organization has established a presence on one service and is now contemplating adding one to additional services. Perhaps you are wondering how you can juggle multiple profiles and still have time left to do other work.

As more and more sales professionals and sales organizations jump on the social networking bandwagon, people are seeking ways to make the time spent on these tools as efficient and fruitful as possible. I recently surveyed several nonprofit professionals and social networking mavens about their social networking habits. The tips below, taken from their responses, offer suggestions for effectively managing your profiles and contacts on social networking sites, finding people with relevant interests to your nonprofit or professional goals, working between multiple social networking sites, and getting the most out of social networking tools even if you're not a web designer or techie.

Invest Time in Networking

While most online social networks cost nothing for your organization to join, keep in mind that creating a strong online presence on one can require an investment of up to two hours a day, especially in the beginning when you are learning how to use the site, setting up your profile, and making friends. If you're unprepared to make this commitment, you may want to consider outsourcing the fundamental set-up of your presence.

Let's face it, Facebook is fairly easy and is by far the largest social networking site; yet what few people realize is that there are over 200 social networking platforms and virtually all of them are searched by the search engine spiders. Having a presence on several diverse social networking sites can raise your web ranking and visibility.

If you don't have someone on-staff who can help manage your social networks, you may want to seek outside help. I suggest finding a social networking intern or an assistant who can spend a minimum of 5 hours per week managing your site or sites.

Test the Waters with an Individual Profile

If finding someone to be a dedicated or part-time social networker for your organization is unrealistic, you may want to consider testing the waters with an individual, rather than an organizational, profile. Whereas creating an organizational presence — such as a group, cause, or fan page — requires a bit more time and planning, setting up an individual profile is fairly simple.

Think of your social networking profile as an online version of the professional networking you might do offline, like attending a conference or a reception. You can connect with peers or potential business contacts, while having the advantage of being able to see their connections — which are not always visible in, say, real life or through exchanging business cards.

An individual profile can also be easier to unplug if early exploration proves unfruitful. You can always delete or make your personal account inactive, whereas it can sometimes be harder to delete a failed group.

Establish a Routine

Many sales professionals say things like, "If am not careful when I go to a social networking site, I am easily distracted. And I know I'm not at all unique."

If you don't organize your time well, establish a disciplined work routine, or have some specific goals in mind when you visit a social networking site (and particularly if you are managing more than one), you will waste time moving from one site to another. Also, work on your own time. Don't feel like you need to keep your profile updated every minute or have to add people to your list of friends the moment they ask.

Don't Spread Yourself Too Thin

There is considerable crossover among social network users, meaning it may not be necessary to maintain a profile or support a group on every single one. Choose where you really want to develop your community and where you really want to interact with the people who matter the most to you and your organization, or use a service like HootSuite.com to manage all of your social networking profiles from one easy-to-use interface.

Share the Workload

You can also involve more teammates by inviting staff members to use their personal profiles to represent the organization. I like to look at social networking as an ecosystem: when you have a number of people picking up different niches, the system is stronger and healthier. Most of the time, you are your best advocate. The more people are involved from your organization, the greater the impact, and without a personal touch these social networks become bland very quickly.

Keep It Personal

People love having an actual person to connect to from an organization, and two-way communication is what makes social networks so successful. You should have your own approach to adding to your list of contacts, or "friending," on social networks.

Well-known blogger and social media guru Ron Jenkins accepts all friend requests, for example, while social media expert and author Mark Williams prefers to establish a connection first by sending potential contacts a private message. Other organizations approve friends based on their personal, professional, or organizational goals.

Yet keep in mind that the goal is not necessarily to amass a large number of friends, but to build meaningful relationships. The task of approving people as friends shouldn't be viewed as a mechanical task of simply clicking a button to add them to your list. It is important to get to know the people in your community. What are their interests? Why did they befriend you or join your organization's group? How can you engage them in a conversation about your organization or sales process?

Automate Profile Content from Blogs, Web Sites, and Other Sources

Not all of the content that appears on your social networking site needs to be created there; as mentioned before, many sites offer tools to allow you to pull in content from your web site or blog, or from others around the web. Facebook allows you to pull in all your RSS feeds from other services. When you update your blog, or your podcast, or your Twitter, it's published to your Facebook profile, too.

"In order to become the master, the politician
poses as the servant."
Charles de Gaulle (1890 - 1970)

Chapter 9 – Web Mistakes You Shouldn't Make

How to Block Your Customers

I believe many sales professionals completely miss the point of
email, and it's costing them business. First, let me establish the
fact that I do not enjoy receiving spam email. I have several
websites with my email address posted throughout the Internet,
so I receive a ton of spam. It's not uncommon for me to receive
somewhere between 200 and 600 emails every day.

About 95 percent of the emails are spam, so unsolicited email has
a daily impact upon my business. I understand that, but I also
understand that receiving unsolicited email is a fact of life. Just
like receiving advertising in my office mailbox each day, it's not
going to stop; and frankly, it shouldn't.

I'm amazed by the response many sales professionals have taken
to prevent unwanted email. Many act as if receiving spam email
is virtually destroying their business, and there is nothing more
important than stopping it in any way possible. They erect barrier
after barrier to insure no piece of email ever hits their desktop as
if the computer would blow up if it did. Unfortunately, the filters,
barriers, and spam blocking services also have a tendency to
block something else: your customers or, worse yet, potential
customers.

When a prospect sends you an email and then receives a message back that says something like, "Hello, I'm protecting myself from unwanted email. Please enter your name in the box below to prove you're a human. Once that is done, I will receive your email."

Forget for the moment that the potential customer may not see your return message (because it may get lost in their spam filter), but what are you really saying to the prospect? I believe when a prospect receives a spam filter message like the one above, he or she thinks, "Wow, it's more important for this company to save 15 seconds of time than it is to see my message. I'm not a spammer. These guys are crazy." Off they go, never to contact you again.

The spam filtering services have a place. They are great at protecting personal email boxes for individuals who don't know how to do it themselves. For the average sales professional, a spam filter service that blocks you from your potential clients until they are cleared is nonsense. It is not incumbent upon the prospect to get your permission to send you a message.

Remove the spam blockers and set up some common sense filters that every email program offers. Then, spend 5 minutes a day clearing your messages and get on with marketing your business.

I'm going to give you an opportunity to save some time and not read the rest of this chapter. Here's why: If you're like me and want to spend the majority of your time closing sales and working with prospects, you don't have time to design a website.

You can spend your day making money and let someone else do the work by visiting www.EvansSalesSolutions.com. Ok, the shameless plug is over. Let's get on with it.

"I Don't Care – I Won't be Back" Rule

It's a hard reality that many people couldn't care less about your website—the same website that you spent thousands of dollars and hundreds of hours developing. Many people will visit and then leave your website without thinking twice about it.

While there's always the dream that your customers will form an emotional attachment to your business, reality is that, in most cases, an emotional attachment never develops. Therefore, it's important to remember what the purpose of your website is; and while I understand that it's very hard for some people not to form an emotional attachment to their own website, you need to always remember that your customers probably couldn't care less. Your web visitors want good information in an organized manner, delivered quickly, and they'll be happy. They're not going to go to bed and dream about your website no matter how much money you spent or how many hours it took to develop it.

One major point to remember is that your website is not your brochure. I understand this sets a normal thinking on its head, but it's true. Think of it this way: if you visit a website once and receive most of the information you need, then you go back and visit that page a second time a week later and the information is the same, what are the chances you'll return to that website a third time?

Statistically, we know that there's no chance of someone returning to your website more than twice if the information doesn't change. It's important to update your website and, at a bare minimum, rearrange the information so that the site always looks new and fresh. One of the biggest mistakes made, particularly by smaller mom-and-pop businesses, is posting the information on the web and then leaving it. It's important to provide accurate and timely information, but it's equally important to provide a wide range of information that changes regularly.

Four-Second Rule

No, this isn't the four- or five-second rule that we've all come to know when we were kids and dropped something on the ground just as we went to place it in our mouth. This is the four-second rule that applies to your website as your prospects or customers are about to make a decision on how long they're going to spend looking at your information.

You should be able to look at the home page of any site and figure out what the site is about within four seconds. If you can't, the site is a failure. People simply don't have enough time to try to ascertain what it is you're trying to do with your website.

I find it amazing how many sales professionals miss the mark and don't understand that their website should be designed to do exactly what direct mail does—that being to motivate people to contact you for more information. I've seen hundreds of sales professionals put so much information on their website that it's impossible to tell exactly what they do. The result is their page is cluttered and presents so many different concepts that any prospect would be confused.

Then, that same sales professional spends several hundred dollars to have their website optimized so that they can get to the top of the search engines. While it's true that if you're at the top of the search engines, you will have more visitors, it doesn't mean you will have more sales. A poorly designed page will be viewed; it just won't make you money. Take an honest look at your website and decide if in four seconds or less you can tell what you do.

"I Designed It Myself" Rule

It seems many sales professionals have a tendency to design their websites themselves. Just because you have the ability to buy programs that will allow you to design web pages, it doesn't mean you should do it. There's a reason why people go to school to learn web design.

A bride can buy a camera and have her friend shoot pictures at her wedding, but the results will be different than if she had hired a professional photographer. Professional photographers hate the idea that someone has such little respect for what they do that they would consider an amateur's work to be as good as their own. However, many professional photographers still feel perfectly comfortable selecting their images and making a website even though they know next to nothing about web design. As a professional salesperson, you must have a web presence, but your page should be professionally designed.

I understand that many web design organizations are a little more than people who purchased a computer and present themselves as professionals, but that's not to say that there are professionals available, who have for years studied how to create the best possible web page. It's your job to find someone who is professional and allow him or her to enhance your business by creating a professional website.

Try Elance.com for hundreds of great web designers.

"What the Heck Is That?" Rule

The "What the Heck Is That?" Rule is simple. If a prospect comes to your website and sees anything on your page that makes them say, "What the heck is that?"—you lose.

For some reason, many sales professionals believe that cursors with fancy tails or humorous pictures of their pets are things that the bride might be interested in seeing. Nothing could be further from the truth, and this type of distraction on your website will only serve to limit your website's success. Here are some of the things to avoid on your website:

Dancing cursor tails of any kind
- Family pictures
- Pet pictures
- Silly playful buttons
- Cartoon images
- Bloopers
- Dishonest claims
- Unbelievable claims
- Phony offers
- Back button blocking
- Accepting payments on an unsecured page
- Phishing for information
- Pop-ups

The "I'm Lost and Can't Get Out" Rule

I'm amazed that what seems like such a simple idea appears to be misunderstood by so many sales professionals. Many times, as I'm surfing the web, I come to a website that will provide me an opportunity to navigate deeper into the page, yet will not provide me with an opportunity to navigate away from the page. There seems to be some belief that by forcing me to stay on their web page for a longer period of time, I'm going to become more inclined to purchase their product. Obviously, the longer I'm forced to be on a page when I want to go to another page, the more frustrated I become. In my particular case, I become much less likely to order products or, for that matter, ever visit their website again.

For me, nothing is as frustrating as getting the information you need or the information you want, and then not being able to use the back button to leave the page. Each time I click on the back button and find I can't leave that web page, the more determined I become to never do business with that business.

Think of it this way: Someone visits your home. You have a great visit. They spend a couple hours with you, and you become friends. You then have an opportunity to convey information to them that you wanted them to have. Then, when they decide to leave, they discover that you have locked the front door and they cannot get out. How long do you believe that they would be your friends?

I'm amazed that there are actually people in the world who believe that by locking me into their web page I will do business with them. It simply doesn't work; it's bad business and should not be done.

Navigational Failure Rule

The navigational structure of your website is the backbone to providing the information your client or prospective client may need. If you don't have a clearly defined navigational structure, people are going to get lost. In the world we live in today, people will not invest the time it may take to figure out what you had in mind when you designed the page. They're not going to fight with a messy navigational structure; they're simply going to go to another page.

One of the most common mistakes made regarding navigation on a website is having different types of navigation structures and buttons within the same site and having poorly worded links so the visitor doesn't know where he or she should go. My favorite saying to my staff when we're developing a web page is that we need to "do it with crayons," meaning it has to be so simple that virtually anybody can understand where it goes.

Your kids may love to play Marco Polo and spend hours each day splashing around a pool with their eyes closed, but I'll bet the average prospect doesn't want to take a course in stellar navigation to find their way through your website.

Another common problem that doesn't get much attention is the order in which your buttons appear. Many times, particularly with organizations where the people who visit the website are familiar with what that organization does, there is a tendency to build the link structure based on needs and not on any common structure you find across many different sites. For example, in the middle of many pages, you run across a picture or certain parts of the picture, that are, in fact, links to other pages. You move your mouse across the image, and as you move from the head to the torso to the feet, different links pop up so that you can go to different pages. While this is fairly cool, it's very confusing to people who haven't visited your website before.

It's much more efficient and provides an easier user interface if you create a link and buttons structure that remains consistent throughout your site. The more trouble it is for someone to navigate through your site, the more chances you will have that they will never visit your site again.

The Too Much Rule

Yes, it's called a web page, and a web page can have quite a bit of information. However, that doesn't mean you have to cram all your material on one page. It's very easy to keep adding material to your home page until it gets out of control.

With so much content vying for attention, it's difficult for the eyes to find the focal point. People get confused, and they leave. A long web page means you have failed to organize your site properly. It probably represents a combination of not planning your site and poor navigation.

The Abracadabra Rule

Don't confuse web design with a magic trick. In a magic trick, you show the audience your right hand and perform the trick with your left. In web design, you tell them where you're going first— and then go there. People have expectations about websites, and they don't like surprises. It will certainly confuse them, and it could make them want to leave and find a site that's less confusing.

If you're a photographer, your visitors expect your website to look like it belongs to a photographer—not to someone who is going to the thrift sale.

Speaking of magic tricks, links should be clearly labeled so your visitors won't be surprised when they click on them.

If you use a vague link description or just say "Click Here" and don't tell people where they'll end up, they could be horribly surprised when they click the link.

If I Build It, They Will Come

Simply having a page on the web isn't enough to attract visitors. You need to continually promote your page on all literature and advertising that you participate in. If you do not promote the page everywhere, nobody will know about it.

When you post your page, you should start funneling all activity through the page. When a prospect needs information, don't mail it; put the information online. When they want to see samples, put them on your page. The best way to increase the activity on your page is to first make sure the information is valuable, usable, and on point. Then make your website the center of your promotional universe.

"They say hard work never hurt anybody,
but I figure why take the chance."
Ronald Reagan (1911 – 2004)

Chapter 10 – Bringing It All Together

Reaching your goal may require some drastic changes to the way you sell your product. I'm confident that the rewards will far outweigh the challenges, and having more income and profit will provide you and your family with the benefits you deserve for taking on this challenge.

Let's do a quick recap:

1. The amount of money you put in your checking account is directly related to the number of sales you make.

2. The amount of sales you make is directly related to the number of presentations you perform.

3. The number of presentations you perform is directly related to the number of face-to-face visits you set.

4. The number of face-to-face visits you set is a direct result of the number of times you ask a prospect to visit with you.

Also,

A = Automation
S = Use a System
E = Education
C = Consistency
R = Repetition

E = Experiment

T = Track Your Work

Now that you know the secret, you're on your way to higher sales but in the event that you do need additional assistance, be sure to communicate with me directly by telephone or email at www.EvansSalesSolutions.com.

Until we have an opportunity to talk again, Good Luck, God Bless, and Happy Selling!

Online resources for sales professionals:

Evans Sales Solutions – **www.evanssalessolutions.com**
Dale Carnegie – **www.dalecarnegie.com**
The Sales Board – **www.thesalesboard.com**
Tom Hopkins – **www.tomhopkins.com**
Tony Robbins – **www.tonyrobbins.com**

Made in the USA
Charleston, SC
04 September 2011